I0098970

# THE UNIVERSAL GUIDE TO LIFE

## A Manual To Help You Maneuver Life's Obstacles

MARKEY L. WALKER

Typist: Patricia T. Shannon, Brick, NJ
Cover art: B-Unique Graphics, Lansing, MI
Production: U.S.A.

Copyright © 2018 by Markey L. Walker

All rights reserved.

No part of this book may be reproduced in any form, by photostat, microfilm, xerography, or any other means, or incorporated into any information retrieval system, electronic or mechanical, without the written permission of the copyright owner.

All inquiries should be addressed to:
Demigod Publishing, LLC
11811 North Freeway, Ste. 500
Houston, TX 77060

This publication is designed to provide information on the subject matters covered. It is sold with the understanding that the author, nor publisher, is not engaged in rendering professional services. If advice or other expert assistance is required, the services of a competent professional person should be sought.

ISBN: 978-1-7321120-0-1 (pbk.)
ISBN: 978-1-7321120-2-5 (ebook)

Library of Congress Control No.

# DEDICATION

This guide to life manual is dedicated to my grandmother Elnora Roland. In all truthfulness, it is she whom I credit for everything it is that I have shared and tried to teach you all here. To me there has been no better teacher in regards to life's lessons, and I only wish that I could rewind the hands of time so I could show her that I not only fully understand all that she was trying to hand down to me (really all of us, only I required special attention), but just how effective I can be at exercising it. And since we all know that is impossible, I am doing the next best thing, which is handing the core basis of what she instilled in me down to you all, in her honor. It will also be nice just to have her hold a copy of this in her hands, even though she will not quite understand what it actually is or represents. Here's to the greatest woman I have ever known.

# CONTENTS

# ACKNOWLEDGMENTS

In addition to my grandmother, I also would like to make acknowledgment and give thanks to my parents Martha and Neil Thomas, the late Sidney Black Sr., my late great-aunt Tinnie Harris, my aunts Tommie Jane "Sue" Chester, Mary "Louise" Walker, Judy Thomas, and Mary Alice Roland, my uncles Curtis Chester Sr., Eugene "Gene" Moore, and the late Willie "June Bug" Hammond. I also would like to specially thank all of the women who have played active roles in my life, along with the few true friends I ever had and every individual who ever aided and assisted my cause, no matter how big or small your efforts or the final results. It is all of you who enabled me to exercise and refine all of the things I needed to, and for you all I will remain forever grateful. Ironically I am also thankful for all who opposed me or my cause, because without them I would not have been able to get the hands-on knowledge of dealing with opposing forces.

# FOREWORD:
# THE UNIVERSAL GUIDE TO LIFE
## "A manual of life lessons and solutions"

In creating this manual I think that if it were left to me, the very first tip would be to simply enjoy life to the fullest while you can! In fact this would probably be my only rule. However, this is bigger than me, and with that being the case, I cannot just simply say go enjoy life and disregard all of the rules and fundamentals that will actually help you to enjoy an (hopefully) easier life.

With this understood, my resolution was and is to remove the notion of "Enjoying Life" as a rule but in turn to make it my first and most important piece of advice. Enjoy life to the fullest while you can. Do not be in a rush to live and be extremely careful not to take for granted the little things, as you will soon see... our calculations or interpretations of time, in that regard, are extremely off! Whereas we are once so eager for time to pass, it will not take long for us to dread how quickly the days fly by, since rarely will we accomplish all that we set out to in a single one.

Now I will not do much elaborating on the tips that this manual will embody, being that they shall be rather self-explanatory. What I will do is explain to you why it is that I have taken the time to draft and spell out to you these rules of engaging in life. Before I do this, though, I would like to stress something which is absolutely necessary that you understand and respect! This manual has not been created for everyone's access and/or use. Neither it in itself nor what it contains is to be shared freely with just anyone, as not everyone is seeking or is prepared for self-betterment.

With that understood, this manual is more like a guide. It isn't going to teach you how to live life but will instead help you to identify the qualities, skills, and abilities that you already possess and will help you to exercise them at will. This in turn will not only enhance your state of being, but should also elevate your quality of living along with those closest to you (i.e., family, loved ones, and friends). To have your eyes opened and your awareness heightened will give you an advantage your peers lack. To have your knowledge peaked and your well of wisdom tapped into early will give you a power you never knew that you could possess! Yes, this shall be your book of life.

In closing I must inform you, then warn you. I want to inform you that like with all things that can bring out the best of you, just reading or knowing about these things are not going to do the trick alone. You have to study, understand, and most importantly... exercise them regularly. Be conscious of them as you maneuver through your daily life. Apply them as constantly as possible, until doing so becomes natural to you. It is at this point that you will notice you have allowed yourself to become one with yourself, and subsequently evolve into the better you that you always knew existed somewhere deep down inside of you. Still the same, never cease to brush up and/or remind yourself. Stay abreast and up to speed until you're absolutely unequivocally positive that you can identify and adapt to each and every element of this guide as it flows through your veins!

As for my warning to you, it is a very simple one indeed. As with anything that gives you the advantage of out-thinking, out-maneuvering, and out-doing those around you... it must be controlled. Failing to control these thing can, without question, prove to be deadly. Make no mistake about this. Another significant fact to take heed to is this... there will be others (seen and unseen) who will take notice and dislike it as well as you with such a passion, that they will literally go to whatever lengths necessary to control it or you, or simply bring about your demise. So be cautious, and control yourself with what you learn while being sure not to allow it to control you.

With that, may you find enjoyment in identifying something new within yourself each and every time you pick this up for a read! May it not only help you to progress and prosper, but may it also assist you in assuring that the knowledge you gain continue to grow strong and live for many generations to come, creating tools and financial stability that will, without question, be needed for their survival, just as it is for ours today.

Best Wishes,
Markey L. Walker Sr.

# 1 SELF-PRESERVATION

*The first law of nature.*
—English Proverb

The reason this has been selected as my starting point is because if you fail to preserve your life, then obviously the rest of this manual will be of no use to you. The fact is that most of what will follow is designed to not only help you to preserve your life, but to try and assist you with accomplishing the necessary feats to help you achieve a higher quality of the life you preserve.

What I like most about this, which is known as the first law of nature, is the fallacy of its true meaning. Self-preservation does not mean to be selfish in order to survive. Yet this is exactly what most perceive it to mean. In all actuality, it simply means to protect yourself from harm or death, and usually regarding the utilization of your instincts.

Now that we have a somewhat better knowledge of what self-preservation really means, let us go over a few things that would be required to exercise doing so:
- A. Learn to understand your instincts.
- B. Practice following your instincts, until it becomes natural to you.
- C. Learn to trust in your instincts.

You will achieve the above by taking time to pay keen attention to what your inner voice is telling you, especially during those times it's speaking to you with no nonsense and your acute awareness kicks in. Get to realize these instances and the reasoning for them coming about when they do. After you've gotten a sense of the how, when, and what... you'll start adjusting your way of reasoning with your inner self, at which time you're to learn how to purposely accept the less perilous option being provided to you by your brain's frontal lobe. You are then to analyze the results of your practiced experiences, and either compare them with potential pros and cons, or maybe even actual situations, to support or dispute the factual results. Once you've made it this far, I am rather optimistic that it will be clear to you, not only the extreme importance of the law, but that it is necessary for you to trust your instincts, so that you may preserve your life.

Does this mean you are to spend your life being afraid to live outside of the box, or be adventurous? Of course not. So do not overdo it and force yourself to start living an overly cautious life. The basis here is simply to help you become more aware, and to make wiser decisions due to your heightened awareness.

Does it mean that you abandon others just because the opportunity presents itself and it may very well preserve your life? Not necessarily. As fate would have it, sometimes it will actually be in one's best interest to preserve life by first aiding others in the preserving of their own. Though this is not an invitation to go out and try to be a hero either, as those situations, more times than not, usually end up in news coverage of their dates with fate as opposed to meeting with the mayor, shaking hands, smiling while ribbons are being pinned on.

# 2 ESTABLISH YOUR ETHICS

*Ethics are necessary, as at the end of
the day they will help define you.*
—M.L. Walker Sr.

I knew very well what ethics meant, yet I searched through several dictionaries until I saw it defined how I would like you all to remember it. Per *Merriam-Webster's Dictionary and Thesaurus*, ethics is defined as 1: A discipline dealing with good and evil and with moral duty; 2: Moral principles or practices. Now take a second and let that sink in.

Of course you are asking yourself why would I ask you to let the definition sink in, because you too know what ethics means. Well, my reasoning is because knowing what the definition of ethics is and truly understanding it are two completely different things. And until you are fully able to have discipline dealing with good and evil, and do so with moral duty... your moral principles and/or practice shall be questionable. The late Samuel Butler's take on morality was this: "Morality is the custom of one's country and the current feeling of one's peers. Cannibalism is moral in a cannibal country." Interesting, isn't it. The fact of the matter is that he was not only absolutely correct back then, but is still so to this very day. Makes one thankful that we weren't born or raised in a cannibalistic country (at least not in the literal sense, as mankind is devoured by one another at an alarming rate in many different fashions).

My overall point is that we all must set out individually to establish our ethics. Will ours at times mirror others? No doubt about it. This will be especially so with those whom we are frequently around or share many other things in common with; however, it will not always be the case. In some cases they may appear to be identical all the way up to certain points or aspects. These certain points or aspects may at times be so minute that they are hardly recognizable; then there will be those which make all the difference and will make all concerted ethics, morals, and principles appear to be like night and day! Nonetheless, the process of establishing them must be completed—unless, that is, you'd prefer to have none.

For me, this process began with a period of self-evaluation. I personally did it all mentally but do feel free to take out a piece of paper, draw a line down the middle, write good on one side and bad on the opposite, and get to writing. Your objective should be to note 2 to 7 things you like or do not like about yourself, the way you carry yourself, or the way you deal with others. At the end of these columns, note what it is that you would like for people to say about you once your life's journey has run its course, and what you wouldn't like for people to say. And NO, this is not about getting people to like you but rather finding a medium on the scale of good and bad to the point whereas there could be many things about you that others honestly could dislike, but on the same breath they would have to admit that there is still something about you that they and others just have to respect!

Okay, so once you have your list compiled, your next task will be to begin figuring out any and all things that may need to be tweaked. Once you've identified all that you feel may need tweaking, begin making small goals for yourself to either start or stop doing. For instance, let's say one of your problem areas is that it is hard for you to make decisions and especially so when it pertains to others. You would first start by being conscious of when these moments or opportunities arise. You would instruct yourself that a decision has to be made and it has to be made by you, and simply make the most rational decision you can make without delay. Will they always be correct? Not in your wildest dreams, but your confidence and ability to make independent decisions will grow, and before you realize it, you will find yourself becoming a quick thinker when put in positions where decisions need to be made. And lastly, you will come to realize that when others are involved... the main thing is simply to be fair as one possibly can be, and that when those situations are impossible, the decision you make is one you yourself will be able to stand on and live with.

Now let's say, for instance, that it's a good moral principle you are dealing with. You give to any and everyone you feel is in need and cannot seem to help it, because you know in your heart it's the right thing to do. The problem is that by constantly doing so, it is now causing a strain in different areas in your own life. Clearly something would have to give, and by you identifying this as an area of attention, you would then set goals to assist you in better handling of situations of this nature. For example, instead of trying to help everyone, you may create a list of certain cases as well as to what extent you will be willing to help. Or you may even find alternative methods of being of assistance to those in need, all the while maintaining not only your contentment of being helpful, but a roof over your own head and clothes on your back. Henry Mere's view of ethics was, "the art of living well and happily." And it is my opinion that he too was absolutely correct, as the ethics you establish for yourself should, if nothing else, bring about the contentment in your life that allows you to rest well at night, knowing that your moral principles are in good standing.

The following are a number of other key components I am in firm belief are inescapable of not being overlooked when structuring your ethical presence. I will address them in their individual capacities so as to ensure your understanding of each one's significance to this chapter.

## PRACTICING LOYALTY

Although loyalty is touted by many in this day and age, not nearly as many actually possess this quality. We hear it so often because, like with so many other things in life, people learn to talk the talk, and some even the walk. So yes, most will speak the loyalty language, and some will even walk it well, but beware! Deception lurks near. For many their only goal is to infiltrate and perpetrate frauds. Let not this be the case with you. Commitment and faithfulness is not as hard to adhere to and exemplify, as those who lack the willpower would have you believe. In fact they can be extraordinary pillars. The key is this:

A. Do not be a pretender;
B. Only commit to whom or those things you truly believe in (sometimes it's necessary to do extra research before doing so);
C. Do not be easily swayed; and
D. Never be first to betray those or that which you have proclaimed your loyalty to.

I will be first to tell you that being loyal will usually cost you more than it will ever earn you; nevertheless, this is the price we pay to truly possess this quality! This is the price we pay to differentiate ourselves from the imposters who only talk it and pretend to walk it but do not live it. It is the price, howbeit a meager one, to remove even the possibility of anyone to question the integrity of what we represent!

## VALUE YOUR WORD

Your word is a direct representation of you (the person you are and what it is that you stand for), and therefore you should do everything in your power to make sure you treat it as such! This should be one of the most important things you ever remain conscious of, because your word will only mean to the next person what your word means to you. And this is why your word should mean absolutely EVERYTHING to you!

Now I know the first thing that comes to mind is how sometimes we mean good when we say the things we do or agree to some of the things we agree to, and then life happens and we simply find ourselves in positions whereas we are no longer able to keep or stand true to our word. Well, that's totally understandable, yet there are remedies and/or preventive measures for even that.

The following are a number of things that you should keep close in mind and heart. These simple pointers will hopefully assist you with ensuring that your word is worthy of closing a million-dollar deal without a red cent needing to be sitting on the table before you. They are as follow:

    A. Never speak just because you have a voice;

    B. Choose your words carefully (think just a little before speaking);

    C. Say what you mean and mean what you say;

    D. Never agree to things when you are unsure;

    E. If unsure, then let this be known;

    F. When agreeing but unsure, cover alternatives;

    G. Once your word has been given, stand on it with your life;

    H. Once your word has been given, if things fall apart, communicate such immediately;

    I. When things fall apart, while communicating such, be prepared to rectify the situation if necessary and possible; and

    J. Never forget that words build AND destroy!

Study these points and keep them close in mind, so that every time you open your mouth you will know exactly which point it is what you are about to say relates to. When you speak, you want people to not only listen, but to feel what it is you are saying. And when you put your word on something, you want for it to be a seal of certification. You want a person to be able to depart from you confident in the fact that you have spoken, and nothing more need be said. If you said it, then it has to be true; if you agreed to it, then it would, without question, be (as long as it was left up to you and life did not intervene!). If words are the only things that last forever, as one William Hazlitt was once quoted as suggesting... what would you want yours to reflect?

## HONOR YOUR OBLIGATIONS

There are many different ways that we may find ourselves becoming obligated to someone or something, be it via agreement, promise, or morals (some would even say law; however, I have my own interpretations of this aspect which will be discussed later in this manual). The thing is this: no matter how we find ourselves becoming obliged, we have an ethical duty to honor our obligations.

Yes, at times, we may not like the idea or may not feel as if we should have to. Maybe someone else failed to before and now we feel the favor should be returned. Unless such instances were or are a blatant disregard or done out of intentional disrespect (in which cases you would be fully excused for returning said dishonor, if that so happened to be your choice), then your obligations should always be honored, if it is in your power to do so.

The honoring of obligations is the proper exercising of etiquette. It exhibits character and helps distinguish you from the average ordinary Joe who goes through life senseless to the extreme importance of displaying this virtue. As discussed in the previous section "Value Your Word," these actions, or lack thereof, will be, and without question are, a direct representation of you, who you are as a person and what you truly stand for! So separate yourself from the pack, be daring to overlook the little things, and jump at the opportunity to be one of the greats to whom the masses will be forced to nod their heads and tip their hats, as the aura of honor surrounding you shall force them to do so. Yes, there will be many so bitter with envy that they will try to restrain doing so, but if you watch closely... even they will give it up. Your presence will demand it.

## DO NOT ASSOCIATE PRINCIPLES WITH FINANCES

Have you ever seen someone with more than enough money, weren't arrogant nor stingy with it, but still no one actually cared for or respected the person? Well, nine times out of ten, this was probably because that person lacked moral principles. Yes, others may still accept the handouts, may even act cordially when in said person's presence, only it would be plain as day one's true position, without jealousy or envy even being a part of the equation.

The point being made here is that you can never allow yourself to become confused with the notion that your financial status is a representation of your moral principles. Money may be able to buy a lot of things, but never has it nor ever will it be able to purchase principles. And in the examples where it appears to have done so, ask yourself... did it really? Because sure as the sun shall rise and set, when the next highest bidder arrives, you will see just what that person stands on and stands for. Men and women are bought daily, but are these men and women worthy of being called your comrades?

In conclusion, just be cautious never to allow the lines to blur. Never fall under the illusion that money will create or repair principles. Only you, your commitment and dedication, will create moral principles and the ethical representation of yourself that you so desire. Also, be leery of any and all who make it evident that their supposed moral principles can be swayed with a dollar bill.

## STAND ON YOUR MORALS

Once your morals have been established, remain steadfast to them as long as they are what you believe in. This will not always be easy, since there will always be opposing forces working to convert you or simply strike you down off your square altogether. This all reverts back to the negative and positive of the scales of life, and thus existence of these forces of opposition will not only be consistent, but shall forever remain. And this is why you must remain strong in your moral conviction and not be easily deterred or swayed.

# 3 TAKE CARE OF YOUR BODY

*The body of man is a vessel and only will be that*
*for a short while before the spirit moves on.*
—M.L. Walker Sr.

Now before we get started, I want to make a few things clear. I am not a health fanatic, a fitness guru, or nutritionist. Nor am I a brain surgeon, psychologist, or anything of the sort. In fact I don't claim to be a leading authority in any of those areas or that I am even the best source of advice here. Nevertheless, I am going to share with you what I can, which is what has helped me, and maybe you are able to take from it and figure out a way to accomplish the goal at hand.

## START WITH THE BRAIN

It is my belief that taking care of your body actually begins with the mind. I feel that if we take care of our minds, then our minds will help us take care of the rest of our body. And how exactly does one go about taking care of their mind?

The first thing on my list is to always try to allow your brain the proper rest it needs. It may not be the full eight hours, or maybe not even six; however... you should always try to allow it the down time it needs to clear itself and rejuvenate. The brain is a muscle and like with any other

11

muscle, if you continue to work it without giving it the necessary break, then it will grow fatigued. And just like with any other muscle, once over-fatigued, it is no longer capable of functioning as it usually would and is intended to. Then if still not given the proper attention, it will in fact begin to shut down or lock up. Well, the same thing happens with the brain. Once overly fatigued, your mind begins to wander, your thoughts become scattered, speech drawn and responses incoherent—some of which could subsequently place you in harm's way, as trying to continue about your daily activities under these conditions would be far from healthy. So remember, always rest your brain. Be it through sleep or meditation, allow your brain the down time it needs to recuperate from its constant state of working.

Next you want to try and relieve your mind of all the stress you possibly can. Now surely I am well aware of the fact that it is no easy feat by far to simply relieve your mind of stress and that if I had the remedy to this, I would be a very rich man by now. Yet there are a number of things that can be done to assist you in doing so. As mentioned above, maybe you're the meditating or yoga type. I personally like to find things I am interested in, like music or writing, and I use these as portals to channel my stress relief. Some of you may find lifting weights, playing sports, swimming, getting massages, shopping, or other things as stress relievers. Whatever the case may be, utilize such as frequently as possible, because stress overloads the brain, causing your mind to work three to four times harder than it normally would, eventually running the risk of a meltdown. Also I would like to add doing so responsibly, since a person who uses shopping or other expense-bearing things to relieve stress would not want to do those things so frequently that they end up creating other stressful issues for themselves.

Surely some of you may immediately think about going the self-medicating route. This is something I would have to strongly advise against. No, I am not going to tell you what to do with your leisure time, but rather am informing you that to equate your stress relief with self-medicating is an extremely bad idea! Life is entirely too stressful and would have you literally stuck in a self-induced coma, neglecting things you should be seeing to, falling behind and simply creating even more stressful situations. To top all of that off, the wear, tear, and eventual deteriorating of the mind that comes as the side effects would nullify all that we are setting out to accomplish in this chapter and life itself!

## COMPLETE IT WITH THE BODY

In advising you to take care of your body, my initial thought isn't exercising, as you all may have thought. Instead my focus is on what you allow into your body, and how it is you treat your body. Of course a bit of exercise truly would not hurt, as not only does it help relieve stress, as just discussed, but it helps you to stay physically fit (which is an amazing feeling all in itself). Only for now let's deal with the most important aspects.

### A. WATCHING WHAT YOU INTAKE

This subject matter actually covers a broad array of things; however, we will try to keep it easy to follow by touching on just food and drugs. It is a no-brainer that these are subjects that are discussed pretty much on a daily basis. Be it on television or daily conversation, I am sure one or the other (if not both) are brought up or mentioned in topics of discussion. Keeping this in mind, I will not drag it out by going over the thousand-and-one warnings. What I will say, though, is be modest in your daily diet, and hesitant and extra cautious of any drugs or alcohol you consume. After all, yours and others' lives may very well be at stake! And surely this fact alone has to mean at least something to you.

### B. TREAT YOUR BODY WELL

You know your body better than anyone else (or at least you should). It is always good to pay keen attention to your body, and this is when it is running well just as much as when it is not running so well. It is also good to do things that you know are good for your body, like eating a balanced diet, getting your proper rest, and living a healthy lifestyle.

Quite naturally you would not want to go around bumping, bruising, and breaking your body up. Nor would you want to constantly put yourself in a position for others to do so (unless you are into contact sports or something). Basically you just want to maintain your body to the fullest of your ability. Just as your motor vehicle would need constant care and maintenance to continue getting you around... so will your body. And when your motor vehicle breaks down, you are never afraid to take it to the shop or have someone get under the hood to repair whatever has malfunctioned... so likewise you should not be afraid or hesitant to visit the dentist or hospital when necessary. In fact I would suggest going in for your annual check-ups as you would (or should) take your vehicles for tune-ups or wheel alignments, because the harsh reality of the matter is that if in fact there is something that isn't going right with your body, then you would rather be made aware of this sooner than later, as the earlier illnesses or potential problem areas are discovered... the higher the probability of prevention or cure. Even in a case where there is no cure available (something I hope and pray with everything inside of me none of you ever have to be subjected to), early detection would allow for proper treatment, and most likely an extension of life (if in fact said disease is terminal).

So be cautious, protective, attentive, preventive, and all else that is necessary to help you live a long and healthy life! Love yourself enough to do that.

# 4 CREATE BALANCE IN YOUR LIFE

*The balance which scales symbolize is an indicator of the return to oneness. bringing matter and time and the visible and the invisible into balance.*
—Dictionary Of Symbols

Creating balance in your life is something that most people spend the majority of their lives wishing they could do, when in all actuality it really is simply up to them just to do it and stop the wishing. Without question there is a process involved, yet it is not complicated, as we have been misled to believe. Will the tips I am about to share with you work for everyone? Absolutely not, as you have to first believe that what is to be conveyed is possible, and secondly, be dedicated in the balancing of the scales of your life.

What I can assure you is this: If you do believe and are dedicated and take the necessary steps that will be discussed, it will not be long at all that you begin to see results. Is this a one-time fix for everything type deal? Don't we all wish. Just as with scales, this is a continuous balancing act, and at times may even require the proper gauging be reset, just as scales must be calibrated. However, the more in tune you become with the fundamentals of the process, the easier it will become for you to pull the balancing act off. As the Dictionary Of Symbols expressed, this is about returning to that "oneness of self," bringing your matter (brain/body) and time, and the visible and invisible into balance, thus lightening the loads of daily stress, burden, and hardship, leaving you free to navigate your days, making progress that can be made and being content with that which may have been unable to be made. It is my notion that this "mastering of the scales" will allow you not only to realize a deeper appreciation of life but will allow you to properly enjoy it a bit more while you are at it.

The very first thing that needs to be understood is the fact that the nature of man and woman is dual, with one side being Animality and the other Divinity. This duality which lies within every man and woman is what makes us complete, and it is our duty to recognize, acknowledge, and accept this duality in order to master the balancing act that will be required to live a fulfilling life. Now as you are probably well aware of, there is not and never will be anything easy about balancing between Animality and Divinity, or what is more commonly known as your lower and higher self. It is no secret that giving in to your lower self (Animality) doesn't take much effort at all, just as it is no secret the discipline and willpower it takes to harness the humility required to live your life constantly on high or the standards one would have to live up to in order to actually apply the word divine to their lives and lifestyle.

The following are the basis for which I see to obtaining the above:

KEEP THINGS SIMPLE

"Life itself is not complicated, but rather it is people who complicate it." This saying has stuck with me for quite some time now, and I try my very best to live by it as much as I possibly can. I am not sure where it comes from, or who I may be quoting (so please don't sue me), only it made all the sense in the world to me. So I had to ask myself, if life is not complicated unless we make it such... then how do I reverse this? After contemplating this, evaluating and analyzing past situations and new ones that arose during this time... it became clear to me.

What I came to realize was this: As long as I kept things simple on my part, the complications that arose, or attempted to impede, were usually neutralized a lot quicker and not allowed to grow bigger than what they were or attempted to be. The simpler I kept it, the less complicated the options for resolution were. I will confess that I then applied some things discussed earlier in this manual, as well as some that will be discussed in later chapters.

In addition to my keeping it simple, I also found it very helpful to help, insist on, and/or require others to keep it simple when dealing with me. This required me to be able to assess situations quickly, so that possible complications could be thwarted prior to them ever actually coming into play. This process of cutting the fat off of situations will become as natural as breathing once you continue to work on coming in tune with the process, from little things such as cut errands down to two or three pit stops as opposed to five or six (saving time, money, and energy), to the more serious life-altering situations that can and will be created when complications are allowed to develop and blossom into even greater complications, as they are accustomed to doing. Sometimes this can take place without your knowledge and therefore you are forced to come in and begin cleaning up by cutting the fat and making the situation a more manageable one.

## GET AND STAY ORGANIZED

Let's face it, being organized just is not something that most of us find pleasure in. It's actually funny just how many people have become millionaires off this common flaw of mankind. Now to my surprise, getting organized was not nearly as hard as I figured it would be while growing up, and if you were to set aside a day when you had absolutely nothing else scheduled to do and devote it towards getting organized... then it would not be nearly as hard as you figured it would be. And yes, I know you are wondering where exactly would you begin? Well, when first beginning, you are going to want to make a couple of decisions:

    A.    Do I start with big or small things?

    B.    Do I go with most important or least?

    C.    Which pile will be kept, donated, and discarded?

Now after you have figured the above three things out, you should get straight to work on it. The things that are least important and/or not used on a daily or consistent basis should be stored furthest away. Even still you could file or store these things according to their necessary use or value, for when you do need them (least used or needed further to the back, then the most necessary or frequently used more readily accessible). The things that are most important or commonly needed or used should quite naturally be in a more convenient space, unless for security and/or safety purposes, at which point you would find locations for such to be well hidden.

For documents, photos, and things of this nature, you should also think about scanning and creating electronic files. You may even consider cloud-based services, which have also become rather popular lately. Be it electronic or digital, this way you would have your things safely secured, yet would always be able to quickly access and reference them without having to dig them up (unless the actual hard copy is needed, in which case a bin or fireproof safe or file cabinet should also be considered as an investment). After a while of running things to be stored, this process will become as easy as 1, 2, 3 (scan, file, store). In fact you could even note the place of storage for each hard copy if you like.

Anyhow, the more you put your system to use, the more your brain will adapt to the program and the easier it will be for you to stay organized. See, it is one thing to, quote-unquote, "get organized" and a complete other to actually stay that way. The good news is that it is not hard to stay that way once you've gotten it in place and a system in order.

Basically you just have to stick to the program that you create, and when you catch yourself getting lazy or deviating from the script, punish yourself by getting up from that cozy spot on the sofa in front of the television, or from under the warmth of your comforter, as these things will register to your brain. Next time leave the keys on the hooks by the door or place your phone on the charger as necessary. And just as you would hope... your tomorrows will, at the very least, be less complicated in these areas, as you will not have to scramble to run around looking for your keys that are buried under one thing or another, or trying to get a charge to your phone that will hold you long enough to do one thing or another that you need to. Nor would you have to worry about the other subsequent, complicating delays or inconveniences that would no doubt follow!

## UNDERSTAND HURDLES WILL APPEAR

Never allow yourself to believe that just because you "keep things simple" and/or "stay organized" that hurdles, pitfalls, and complications will not find or make their way into your life. Believe it or not, this is all a very key part of life itself. It's all about you being dedicated to keeping it simple and staying organized, ensuring that the balance you've created in your life remains calibrated!

As you grow in your belief and understanding of identifying factors of these hurdles, pitfalls, and complications... just as you learned to assess the situations and thwart the complications by cutting the fat, you will learn to apply the same techniques here. It is all about knowing how to identify, prevent, and easily resolve any and all things that have or will create an imbalance within your life, and being dedicated to exercising the necessary techniques to help bring about the balance you desire.

## ALTERNATE METHODS

Of course there are many different possible ways for a person to find or create balance in their life. Some people use meditation, yoga, religion, or becoming Naturalists (spending time in nature to try returning to oneness with the earth).

Exercising, massages, spa treatments, and therapists have also been helpful to some. Whatever you find that works for you will be just fine. As long as it is effectively de-stressing your life, then surely it has to count for something.

Stress is as natural as most other things in our lives and is actually a response to alarms our brains set off. The problem is that it is closely associated with a host of ailments. So yes, I guess it will be safe to say that finding or creating balance in our lives very well may allow us to remain mentally and physically healthy, hopefully adding years to our lives.

# 5 MASTER SELF

*To master self is to gain knowledge and*
*understanding of who you truly are.*
*To harness the animal, restrain the betrayer,*
*and assume control of the reins.*

M.L. Walker Sr.

Here is where you will find yourself trying to accomplish one of the hardest tasks ever set before you. If you have read the previous chapters, then you may have noticed how "Establishing Your Ethics" touched on the good versus evil of man in defining ethics, and the balancing act of scales covered in "Create Balance In Your Life." Well, there is a very good reason for this. As you should be very aware of, everything in life revolves around the supreme energy which is balanced by positive and negative. In this text we will look at these energies as "higher self" (positive) and "lower self" (negative).

To explain why accomplishing Mastering Yourself is going to be so difficult, I will start by reminding you of how your mind and body frequently appear to have minds of their own. Yes, your inner voice may try to pull things together for you; nevertheless, how often does that work? And what about those of you who have allowed the opposing voices to both live inside of you? Surely it must be a hassle calming these quarrels.

Either way, what we are experiencing at this time is a clashing of our higher and lower selves. None of us are exempt, never have been nor will we ever be, as the harsh reality is that we have been wired to find enjoyment in living carefree. It's intoxicating, exhilarating, and creates a euphoria that we have grown to love. Indeed our carelessness may come in different shapes, forms, or fashions, yet they are one and the same, no doubt!

Now before I provide you with the tips I have to share, I must first be honest with you. This is the area that will either make or break you! You will either emerge from this chapter knowing that you are on your way to greatness, or you will emerge with thoughts of hopelessness. This is sad, but unfortunately true. I will say this, though: even if it is the latter, I still suggest that you not only finish this read, but that you challenge your lower self, and do so wholeheartedly, with every intentions of prevailing! This is in fact what this chapter is all about, and just because it may come easier to some... don't you be the one to count yourself out! No way, no how. In fact do everything in your power to prove wrong any who you feel have tried or may try to count you out. We are building winners and you must start by conquering the biggest giant you ever have or ever will have to face, which is yourself!

## STUDY YOUR STRENGTHS AND WEAKNESSES

We all have our strong points and weak points. Physically, mentally, spiritually, you name it, the scale is there and the balancing act active. Your job is to start paying acute attention to your strong areas and weak alike. If need be, begin documenting these so as to make it easier to identify and correlate different behavioral patterns that may be attached to said attributes or flaws. The objective is to pinpoint and individualize these characteristics, so that you may examine, analyze, research, and/or whatever else is needed to be known about these (your) attributes and flaws. This way you can figure out what it will take to increase or maintain the strengths in your strong areas, and how to increase strength in your weak areas, modify them or figure out a way to compensate for them wherever necessary.

While studying your strengths and weaknesses, do not forget to assess your gifts as well as your vices. Both of these usually play a major role in who our true selves are, along with the battle between our higher and lower selves. Thus it will be necessary to approach these in the same manner, so that you can learn to nurture your gifts in hopes of preventing them from becoming your curse, and harness or eliminate your vices so they do not become the cause of your demise. Make no mistake about it, we are our own worst enemy! And whoever acknowledged this fact was definitely one of the wisest beings ever (and I do not care what color they were). So do not fool yourself; know that betrayer lurks closer than you could ever imagine, and only you yourself can still be the one with the last say of how that all plays out.

## CONTROL YOUR EMOTIONS

Joshua Loth Liebman was quoted as saying, "Emotion is not something shameful, subordinate or second rate; it is a supremely valid phase of humanity at its noblest and most mature." What in the hell was he drinking, and exactly which planet again was he on?! I mean clearly it was not planet earth.

Seriously though, in some rare situations I can easily agree with this gentleman; however, for the most part and in this date and time, one would be very wise to keep their emotions in check. The ugly truth is that sometimes you cannot even allow certain family members to get a true sense of your emotions or the way they work. There will be more on this in later chapters; however, for now you must be made aware that hyenas of emotions do not discriminate. They are cold-blooded predators and any emotional being is potential prey.

So what exactly am I saying about controlling your emotions, and how exactly do you go about pulling it off? Well, what I am saying is this... when dealing with most people, you have to learn to conceal what it is you truly feel. If made angry, you dare not let it show. Even at times when you are overflowing with joy... to crack a mere smile could turn those tides immediately. And I know, you are figuring, "Wow, it really can't be that serious." Yet I bet each and every one of you, my pinky finger to your dime, that you do not have to think back too far to find an incident where if you were not mistaken, you could have sworn someone you allowed to observe your emotion one way or another actually preyed on it. Exactly, my pocket would be just a-jingling away, because whether it was someone who saw you were too happy and decided it was the best time to crack for a loan (sensing you had gotten that payout you had been waiting for), or the lover who knew how much you hated for them to answer their communication devices during meals, using such to spark the false fight so they can go for a drive to clear their head... the vultures are circling.

Unfortunately, I cannot really tell you how to pull off keeping your emotions in check. Trust I truly am sorry for this. Only the fact is that we all have so many different emotions and they differ in so many degrees, that it would be literally impossible for me to create a formula to control them all. There will be some things later in chapters—"Control Your Tongue," "Master Your Surroundings," "Learn The Art Of Reading People," "Play Your Hand Accordingly," and more—that will be of assistance. Still, the final outcome of this will be left up to you. No one knows your emotions better than you do. No one knows who you feel should be or is trustworthy to be privy to certain emotional states. And lastly, no one but you will be immediate emotional prey for failing to take heed and properly protecting yourself.

Am I advising you to live in a shell? Not at all. What I am advising you to do is gather some self-control over yourself and your emotions, to be cautious of to whom you allow access to certain emotional states, and to be cunning when necessary with those whom you recognize as being hyenas or vultures of emotions. And likewise, you should be extremely careful when other people's emotions are involved, as there is no more deadlier situations than those involving a lack of control of emotions. My mother always told me not to play with people's emotions, and why I shouldn't.

## DO NOT ALLOW THINGS TO CONTROL YOU

This subject could easily fall in with several that have already been covered, as recently as the last, and with more to come. Still in all, it needed to be discussed in its own accord. See, the majority of us spend our lives with things like money, material possessions, food, and drugs actually controlling us every step of the way. And as truth would have it, that same majority of us have no length to which we would not go in pursuit of, or to maintain our stronghold of such. Yes, I too am guilty of this (as I know is the thoughts of those of you who know or knew me personally, or you who have heard of or read about me); however, only to a certain extent. It is true that I have a very intimate and strange relationship with money, was a jewelry fanatic and shopping addict who went through vehicles like the years did seasons. The thing is this: I did not see the millions I could have easily seen as a teenager, as I was not one whose allegiance could be bought, nor could one's misperception of my hunger being greed be preyed upon. No... I was content with how active I was or was not. Still, I was not one who was stingy and would not spread the wealth. Yes, this impeded my growth, yet is simply a testament that I did not sell my soul to the point where I lost my morals and principles. No, no... my ethics remain intact. My shopping sprees were not done alone, and even if I had... I bore gifts upon return. How else could such moments be truly enjoyed? And as for the cars and things... I never had more than a permit, liked being driven, and tired of them easily, so you do the math. Hell, I even let the jewels get away from me from time to time. See, I refuse to let these things control me.

It's up to you to decide whether or not you are going to allow things of that nature to control you. This is something that you should really take seriously, because once you give this control up, it will be hell and high waters trying to regain it. Just look at those who allowed partying to turn into full-fledged addictions. You have people who have literally forfeited the bulk of their lives, if not their life, all because they opted to relinquish that control. You must be wise and remain steadfast in your quest to maintain control over yourself. You are the one with the ability to think and make decisions, and therefore there is absolutely no excuse why you in turn would not be the controller of things as opposed to things being the controller of you. And with this in mind... ask yourself, is it really necessary for me to provide tips here?

DO NOT LET SEXUAL DESIRES CONTROL YOU

I will not try to convince you that sex is overrated, as I sometimes (emphasis on *sometimes*) feel it is, but rather will approach this with the notion that sex is everything that it is cracked up to be, and then some. Let us say, for instance, you never fail to please or be pleased. You're just good, know how to get the job done, and require the same in return. All of this would be just fine and dandy. The problem comes in when it becomes apparent that one has lost control to desires of these acts. Be it male or female, once control has been lost and for whatever reason or excuse... this is or would be, without question, a very big problem.

When a person's sexual desires take control, this person usually finds himself or herself being susceptible to being placed in compromising positions, exposed to venereal diseases at a higher rate, and pretty much a slave to these desires. All of which are counter-productive to everything that we have been going over this far. No, I am not suggesting that you not have an active sex life. If that's what floats your boat, then sail on. What I am suggesting is that you think with your brains and not with what's between your legs. "Think with your big head, not your little one," the Father told me on November 16, 1989... "and you will do just fine." Clearly those words never left me. I will, however, admit that I really did not take heed to them to the fullest at that time and will withhold the response that went through my mind regarding his comment, but over time I realized his point was actually beginning to sink in. Somehow I had to gain and maintain total control of my sexual desires. Under no circumstances could I allow them to control me or surely they would be the cause of my demise.

The more conscious I became, the better I was able to handle situations. For example, in recent years we have witnessed individuals such as Bill Cosby, Harvey Weinstein, Larry Nassar, Russell Simmons, and Steve Wynn (just to name a few) come under fire for supposed sexual abuse and mistreatment of women for sexual gratification. These men, who all had become legendary in their respective fields, fell from grace, losing respect, seats at their own companies, endorsements, honors, and even freedom, because they were not able to control their sexual desires. Donald Trump, however, would still continue to ascend to actually become the President of the United States of America and openly condone behavior in contrast with this sub-topic, yet the wake of exposure of abuse and mistreatment allegations that gave birth to movements such as #METOO could easily be traced back to his presidency. And yes, this chapter still applies to women as well, since any gender can fall victim to sexual vices, only an example dealing with the male species was needed.

So hopefully you get the message I have tried to convey here. Trust me, we all go through the phase of being young, wild, and sex-driven, only do try to use your brains and not allow your sexual desires to control you, subsequently costing you more than you can afford (and I don't mean this in a monetary sense at all). When in different situations, think of it as rolling a set of dice in a smoke-filled room, with everything you possess in the world (your life included) at stake, and someone way on the other side of the table calling out your number rolled. Does not sound fun at all, does it?

## EXTINGUISH JEALOUS THOUGHTS

I am going to give it to you plain and simple: Jealousy is for the weak. The weak at heart, mind, and soul. This is an emotion that you must do everything in your power to rid yourself of. You must put this emotion out once and for all and never allow it a place to live inside of you ever again! Why? Because it is self-defeating, unbecoming, and simply just a waste of such valuable time and energy.

The first thing you need to do is acknowledge your jealous acts or tendencies, as denial and excuses are the usual line of defense. After you have openly admitted to yourself the truth about your jealousy, ask yourself, why is it that you are jealous of this person or that person? Once this part has been established, you will now ask yourself whether or not you could accomplish the same exact thing (or even better) if you truly applied yourself and/or were devoted to acquiring whatever that was? Then you will ask yourself, was there anything better or more productive to your cause that you could have been doing with the time and energy you have given this other person?

The above is just a single exercise that can be used to help you douse the fire of jealousy. Becoming more aware of your self-worth will also be of much help here. The main thing is that you have to be diligent in your efforts to rid yourself of this ungracious trait. You should never want to give others the power of knowing that they have this type of effect on you and are able to evoke such emotional flaws out of you at will, simply by excelling. No, you congratulate them (literally or mentally) and work harder, plan better, think clearer, and let it come as no surprise to you when you shine brighter! This guide will help you do this. Trust me, there were too many occasions to count where I would walk into a room with numerous people and would receive more recognition, love, and respect than guys who it was no secret had two or three times the money or possessions I had. I mean this was insane to me because some of these individuals would actually end up displaying jealousy and envy towards me.

I personally accredit sticking to the script of this guide that I am now sharing with you. No, I did not have a hard copy to grab and reference at will; it ran through my veins and I had to be studious in learning to understand, master, and exemplify.

The power contained within what I am sharing with you is incomparable to anything you have ever known. It's more powerful than money, it's even more powerful than weapons. It's character, class, and the ability to be the bigger person. This, comrade, is priceless and no weapon created could ever be more powerful when executed accordingly.

## NEVER DO THINGS THAT ARE NOT NECESSARY

A lot of times we find ourselves in positions whereas we just do things simply for the hell of it. Some of these things may be minute or insignificant, while others may carry dire consequences. But get this: in this manual they equate to one and the same, something you did that was not necessary.

Yes, I know how it is when we just want to go that extra step in order to make a point, ensure an understanding is reached, or whatever the case may be. Yet if it is not absolutely necessary, then chances are there is really no need to do such. From the smallest to the largest situations, you should apply this to your life, as it is unmistakable the direct connection it has with so many characteristic elements discussed. Save yourself the time, finances, energy, and hassle. Do only what needs to be done as determined by necessity; nothing more, nothing less.

No, this does not mean abort plan B's or C's, as in most cases alternatives are necessary in order to prevent poor performances or failure. This subject is referring to situations which you know have reached their stages of completion. Where you know that there is truly no need to proceed any further with it. Restrain yourself, take a breath, and move forward. Your time, finances, and energy should be things you utilize wisely, and surely we all can do without the pains and hassle.

## KEEP YOUR EGO IN CHECK

Now do I really have to go into a long, drawn-out adage or walk you through the one way to keep your ego in check, or when? If so, then unfortunately I truly do not know what to say. Why? Because this actually should be one of the very easiest and quickest things for you to get in order. I mean, we all know when that little evil twin of ours is itching to creep out and why. And just as well, we all know that ninety-nine percent of the time it honestly is really uncalled for and unnecessary. So in saying this, I am saying, do not be afraid to humble yourself. You and those closest to you know what it is that you represent and are about, and therefore you should have absolutely nothing to prove to anyone. Save the show, and better yet, do not become the sideshow, and if that is not enough, then refer to later chapters of this manual and it will guide you on how to deal with situations accordingly when all else fails. For now, though... master who it is you are!

# 6 SECURE YOUR FOUNDATION

*What you build will only reach as high and
stand as strong as what you build it on.*
—M.L. Walker Sr.

Substantial thought, time, and care should be put into the building and securing of your foundation. This single aspect is of great importance and should in no way be taken lightly. The foundation of your life, or creation of, should be to you the equivalent of an architect's in planning, preparing, and finally the construction of his most durable and long-lasting structure ever created. One built with supreme intelligence, the most advanced technology, and the highest grade of materials. Designed to sustain calamity, be it caused by man or nature.

In a sense, the laying of your foundation has been what you have been studying and working on in the previous chapters. Putting together the foundation on which you, the structure, will stand. Now it is all about securing this foundation, which entails ensuring it is properly supported, has all the proper drainage outlets, and is fit for the bulk of the structure to be constructed according to schedule, to ensure conditions do not change to interfere with such and possibly ruin all that has been accomplished up to that point. And yes, this may even require a few extra precautions be taken to protect it, such as coating it with water repellent, layering the edges and water outlets with gravel to assist against shifting of soil and sinkholes, or you may even erect a fence around the land, as many people do during periods of construction.

Metaphors aside, when building your ethical base, let it be of the highest quality of substance, as this is YOUR foundation. Treat your body with the best care, as this is your structure that has been built upon it, and designed with supreme intelligence. Let the advanced technology of which it runs and operates be well thought out as you set out to master self. May your decor be balanced, responsibly placed in an organized fashion in your own style. And use all else to preserve the life of your structure, and understand very clearly that even the most durable and advanced structures MUST still be maintained! There is no getting around or compromise here; either you maintain what it is that you create and build of yourself... or surely it shall crumble and fall as a pile of rubbish and left to decay. May you keep this close in mind and heart as you proceed, as sometimes we only get one chance to get it right.

# 7 BE ADAPTABLE

*Adapting allows progression to take place and*
*if this were not a natural instinct, surely we*
*would not be far off from the stone age.*
—M.L. Walker Sr.

The ability to be adaptable is what I like to look at as more a craft, and my reasoning is because it just is not as simple as being able to bend this way or that way, when situations or circumstances dictate such. As we have discussed in earlier chapters and will do so more in depth within several to come, a lot of what is required to set yourself apart from the crowd revolves around being able to stand firm, be rigid and unyielding. Albeit, this is not always the case. Just as we are well aware that some firm, rigid, or unyielding objects or materials are only as firm, rigid, or unyielding depending on its environment, conditions, placement, or pressure applied (as the tiniest change in either could make all the difference), the same applies to us as human beings.

So what this mean is this: Sometimes we must have a little give or flexibility within us. That foundation may very well have to sit on rollers to allow it to slide or shift a little in extreme winds or tornados, in order to emerge from the midst of storms, not only avoiding complete destruction, but hopefully doing so with as minimal damage as possible. Or maybe each level of what you construct is done so on its own individual beaming structure, giving flexibility. Either way, it is all a part of your durability set-up.

Now the reason I like to consider this a craft is because as with you (just as with the example above), the average person would not even be able to recognize the imperceptible adaptable measures put in place for the survival of your structure. But the main reason I consider it such is because in most situations there is no easy fix, and therefore circumstances must usually be gauged on their individual bases, and sometimes with precise accuracy being vital!

As expressed, there are no quick fixes or ready-made remedies for the majority of life's twists and turns that would require this craft. Still, there are things that you can do to not only try to better prepare yourself, but to hone your craft. The following are some of the things I have found to be effective in aiding me to be versatile and a bit more universal within my life and interactions with others.

## TRULY UNDERSTAND ADAPTABILITY

The very first thing you must do is seek to truly understand adaptability. Not just the definition but rather the quality of flexibility, liquidity, versatility, and being universal. The greater your understanding becomes, the more it should give way to light that reflects the imperativeness of not only your adding this to your structural application, but your faithful honing of such as well! This is the craft that gives you the ability to think on your toes (making sometimes, but not always, split-second decisions), out-think, outmaneuver, and hopefully outlive those around you. It gives you the ability to think ahead, to calculate situations in real time, and to weather storms of all magnitudes.

Truly understanding adaptability will also open your eyes to many different ways in which it can be utilized in your life and interactions. It should also compel you to learn how to think many steps ahead, plan alternatively, and stay prepared for interjecting with and executing alternative options. To truly understand this is to truly understand that failure honestly is never really an option, as in those cases where such appears to be the outcome... either you are planning on top of planning, or adaptability skills should have allowed you to exit having at least salvaged something to continue on the desired path, or at the very least the reorganizing/rebuilding process. Hence the "all was not lost" and "failure is only one step closer to getting it right" sayings.

## STUDY NEUTRALITY

Neutrality is something that does not come easy. Be it our upbringing or principles that we latch onto later in life... we just figure there's always a side to be taken. And although I am sorry to have to be the one to burst that little bubble of yours, that simply just is not always the case. In fact to be completely honest with you, I personally think it rarely should be the case. My thought on this is that in most situations, the choosing of sides is not even necessary, just the lending of an unbiased ear. Furthermore, unless it is an issue of which you have already chosen a side and/or such is in need of validation, you never want to hastily or inexcusably attach yourself to individuals, beliefs, positions, or causes, since it is very likely that you will be called on such at a later date and expected to stand accounted for! And surely you yourself know that is not a position you would want to be put, or find yourself, in.

Likewise it could very well be an issue that you have long decided which side you stand on, yet the time, place, or company may not require such to be revealed. Either way it is good to learn and even better to practice neutrality. The following are a few techniques that may prove useful:

    A. THE BAILOUT: This is simply expressing that you are clearly in no position to choose one way or the other. You may even suggest it best to let the opposing sides come to agree or disagree on their own.

B.  INDECISIVENESS: This is when you lean towards one side all the way up until the other side comes with their strong point, at which time you switch. It's as simple as acknowledging the strong point and why it is such, and then sliding right off either side. "You both have very good points, so I really can't say... it's hard to decide."

C.  MEDIATOR. This is self-explanatory. Right out the gate you acknowledge you have never been able to really decide one way or the other, then you simply mitigate the strong and weak points, support either side, plus rebut each side. Your intentions would never be to sway either, but simply to help each side agree to disagree.

At times said situations may indeed be physical and would therefore call for action or lack thereof. In my opinion one should still adhere to the aforementioned, and as for the steps to be taken, the bailout or mediator should still apply. The bailout being the washing of one's hands with the ordeal right from the start, if there is no vested interest. The mediator being one to separate or calm the situation at hand, if you have a vested interest and the power to do so. If, however, your side is one that has already been chosen, or your attachment one already etched in stone... then your position has already been set for you, and choices or options are of no existence—you do what is required of you.

If you noticed, indecisiveness was left out in regards to the physical aspect of being neutral. The reason for this is because there will only be action or lack of action, and anything in between will be foolish, as only a clown or numbskull would perform such an act. And furthermore, do not assume that just because you fail to act, this is a choosing of sides, as this is not necessarily so. The situation has to go in someone's favor, or could in fact be evenly balanced. Other times you may interject and then be the mediator a little later. Either way one could never actually attach you to one side or another, unless you yourself act in concert somehow, at which time I guess you will have chosen one (whether unconsciously or consciously).

I gave no specific scenarios because I want you to be able to look at and apply this to pretty much any type of situation, with any type of individual, group, or cause. The art of being neutral is different from being a fence-straddler, as a fence-straddler will very rarely stand on any side, including those to which they have every right and responsibility to do so. The art of being neutral is the art of retaining control of the weight of your opinion, vote, or assistance, whereas straddling fences is the failure and inability to ever stand and be accounted for! It is my position that on this one there should not be any indecisiveness as to where it is you stand, but that there is truly one side to stand on, and it is not on a fence.

## DO NOT BECOME TOO ATTACHED TO PEOPLE OR THINGS

In the previous sub-chapter we spoke on becoming attached to individuals, beliefs, and/or causes. Here what we are building on is slightly different. It is the mental and emotional attachment to not only people but to material things as well. And yes, I understand why and how it may appear as if my advising you all to refrain from becoming attached to people or things is like asking you to go against nature, since that is how naturally we pick up and exercise this deadly flaw. Well, I am here to tell you that over-attachment is in fact what is going against nature. Do you remember earlier when I spoke on the betrayer within you? Here it stands yet again, and as deadly as ever!

The first thing I want is for us to agree on one thing... people and materialistic items will always come and go! No, usually not all, but unquestionably most, correct? Now let me touch on one key word of the subtitle... TOO. It says to not become TOO attached to people or things. See, our minds and emotions have a tendency to work against us, as I asked you to reflect back on personal situations or circumstances directly related earlier in this guide. This is inevitably a core aspect of human nature (always has been, always will be).

Is not this a flaw and is not it fatal? If you were unable to answer yes to both of these, I want you to now ask yourself, how many times have you heard of, experienced, or witnessed situations becoming potentially, or even actually, deadly... all because one (or more) person became overly attached to another person who was not as equally yoked? Be it friendship, relatives (we will discuss the difference between this and family in a later chapter), or intimate partners. Now let us apply this same question with respect to materialistic things. How many times have you heard of, experienced, or witnessed a situation become potentially, or even actually, deadly... all because one (or more) person became overly attached to something material? Be it jewelry, clothing, vehicles, or whatever. The harsh reality is that it happens more frequently than we would like to think. And although I will agree to the fact that some of these individuals are nothing more than mentally disturbed, I would have to say it is far less than you would probably imagine. A temporary insanity is very plausible, only the fact remains that we too can so easily find ourselves on either end of this equation, if we do not refrain from over-attaching ourselves to people or things.

There is no set way to overcome this counter-productive trait, and since we all have our own individual emotional characteristics, it makes it sort of complicated to properly advise on it as well. What I will do, though, is give you the key points to focus on, try to better explain the gauging process, and hopefully this will give you the insight needed to allow you to begin building the capacity to resist. To be honest, at the end of the day resistance is the strongest line of defense that we have.

The first key point is Importance. How important is this person or object to you, and what importance does or would either serve in your life? After answering these to yourself (whom you do not have to lie to or be modest with about it), you will now gauge it. Does this person or thing deserve whatever level of importance you have given it? Is the level of importance even high enough whereas it deserves a place in your life that is reserved for the most important? If it is a person, what would you guess your level of importance is to them and in their life? Once you have answered these, you can move on for now, and hopefully with just a tad bit more clarity.

The next key point is Difficulty. How difficult was it for you to build this relationship or acquire this material item? How difficult is it to maintain and retain? After answering these questions, you will now gauge it. Was it too difficult? Should it have been? Could such be repeated? If you had to do all over again, would you? Is such worthy of the level of difficulty? Is the level of maintenance worthy of such being retained? Once things of this nature have been answered, you can move on, and once again, hopefully with a tad bit more clarity.

See, there are no right or wrong answers with this. This is your life and all you are doing is assessing the people or things in it, and gauging whether or not they deserve to stay there. After you have made a ritual of this, you will learn to do so prior to even attaching yourself in the first place. In fact, the more you go over what's already in your life, a stop or pause indicator should start clicking when something new pops up wanting in anyhow. And no, this does not mean that you just automatically start shutting people or things out of your life, but that you will simply start controlling the level of such more appropriately. Basically some people or things are meant to be there, only they never were meant to be there any time longer than necessary. Whereas other people or things it would be very nice to have around, yet the maintenance and toil would not make such logical, or at least at that particular time. So maybe you plant a seed to see what the future brings. Other things you may very well abort right out the gate altogether. I mean no one wants to attach themselves to a cinderblock and chain right before diving into a lake, as unless you are some type of mad magician... this could only end badly!

As for people or things that do pass your test, then yes, not only do you acquire and maintain them, but you do what you have to in order to protect and retain them. After building up the necessary resistors, your immediate circle of people and most valued assets should be more than maintainable. What you must keep in mind is the fact that even after you have come this far, there still are no easy fixes. You have to continuously monitor and adjust your assessing and gauging. You have to continuously work on staying sharp and not allowing yourself to fall into that overly attaching mode. And yes, I will be the first to tell you that it truly is a job and a half. Yet by the same token, it's a lesson worth its weight in gold a thousand-fold, once you compare it to the flip side. I just hope that you are a bit wiser than I was growing up and not allow the cons to outnumber the pros which you compare them to.

Finally, for the few people or things that you just find yourself incapable of building a resistance up for... some of these people or things are just meant to be, and therefore we accept them or it for what it is worth as opposed to continuing to waste the energy trying to fight it. Just try to practice moderation. Other things that we know truly are not meant, not only should we continue to work on building up resistance, but we should seek assistance and/or attempt different methods in our efforts to do so.

## LEARN NOT TO JUDGE

One of the most important things I feel I ever learned in my lifetime is that we never know what life has bestowed upon the next person. Sometimes it may be a bit more evident than others, but for the most part things are not always what they seem. And as truth would have it, a lot of things are rarely what they seem, and therefore it is usually best if we not only reserved judgement but learned to refrain from judging altogether.

How exactly does this apply to being adaptable, you wonder. Well, let me explain. To judge is basically to form an opinion or to make an authoritative decision on. Now when doing this in regards to people, what we tend to do is put ourselves in a category which we create out of comparison that we immediately do between either ourselves and the other person, someone we know and the other person, our situation and the other person's, and/or someone else's situation and the other person's. Usually after this is done, a side or position has consciously or unconsciously been taken, and once a side or position has been taken, our ability to be adaptable becomes limited. Is the nexus apparent now?

By allowing ourselves to refrain from judging people, we become capable of being able to compare ourselves in a different manner. To be able to place yourself in another person's shoes opens your mind to a humbleness which enables you to, at the very least, empathize with them, and in turn increases your ability to adapt to the situation or circumstances at hand. Even if just for the time being, it puts you in a place where you can comfortably relate, and although it may not be much of a secret that you all came from two very different places or situations... none of that would be of any importance, even if just for that moment.

Honestly there are many more reasons why it is that we should refrain from judging people, only I want to keep this along the lines of adaptability so I tried to stay as far away from them as possible. Most of these reasons I am sure you are already very familiar with, and others will be touched on more in depth in later chapters, as well as the times when we must judge people. As for now, using the art of refraining to judge as a common practice would be a winning method. At times it may even open up doors that you would have otherwise closed for yourself. And in most cases should undoubtedly make the process, after you have entered those doors, a lot easier and more comfortable than it could have and more than likely would have been, had you not humbled yourself to the point whereas judging the next person was no longer nearly as important as coexisting with that person in a world that is in fact made up of so many very different people! All with usually the same simple goal... surviving.

## ACCEPTING CULTURAL KNOWLEDGE

One of the biggest hurdles to conquer in the process of being adaptable is that which comes with cultural differences. The funniest thing about all of this is that we as the human race are more alike and have more in common than any of us would like to admit. In my case I think the transition was relatively easy due to the fact that I had White, Hispanic, Christian, Catholic, Muslim, and you name it, all on the very block I grew up on, and within my family. In fact, on my block there were a couple of preachers, many sinners, health freaks, to the sickly and pretty much everything in between. And this was only on my block alone, so you can probably imagine the rest of the neighborhood and city covered any range that your mind could travel to. And let me tell you... from early on, I was trying to cover every inch of soil of that city I could! And before long I even got the chance to see a few other places, only not nearly as many as my heart desires to see.

Back to the topic at hand. Cultural knowledge is everywhere out there and being offered up on a daily basis. You do not have to necessarily immerse yourself into studies or take courses. Sometimes to merely pay attention to and retain some of the lessons being given or taught by those in position to accurately do so will suffice. For instance, just knowing the customary way of greeting someone could go an extremely long way. Even if that person was or is now utilizing our custom. Or maybe you are out dining and have a dish that you happen to like; something as simple as this could gain an unspoken respect that could pave paths of gold. You just never know what type of positions or situations you may find yourself wanting or needing to adapt to, and by being open to accepting knowledge of yours as well as others' cultures, you give yourself a bit of an advantage. For those whom you may encounter, their first thoughts when presented with a piece of their culture will be that either you have been immersed in the culture in some form or fashion, or simply cared enough to learn about it. Either way, the majority of those you encounter will respect and appreciate the fact or, at the very least, the effort. No, not all, as it's just a given that some people are just negative no matter what, but surely the majority should. And even in the worst-case scenario, the cultural knowledge gained only adds to and refines the person that you already are, and that, my comrade, is worth too many times more than the lesson to count!

# 8 HAVE YOUR OWN STYLE

*Trends will come and go like the wind,*
*but style... now, that can last a lifetime.*
—M.L. Walker Sr.

Some of the many definitions of style are: a way of speaking; a manner or method of acting; a distinctive or characteristic manner; a distinctive appearance; fashionable manner; elegance and sophistication. Okay, so clearly for some of us, being elegant and sophisticated is absolutely out of the question. Not that it's impossible to achieve, but rather that just might not be our cup of tea. The catch is this: Even if your style is rugged and rough... if you are doing so with finesse and gracefulness, then it may still be elegant and very possibly sophisticated, depending on the culture. Anyhow, these are some of the things that we will be building on in this chapter, because it is not about just having style but rather the knack to be able to make whatever style your own.

First things first: when it comes to fashion, please know and understand that it is like almost impossible for any of us to actually create a style from scratch. The fact is that we are so late in the game that the most any of us would be able to do is start a trend. In short, history has seen pretty much every style there is to see, so much as to when it comes time for the space age cultural fashion... the world will be ready. And there will be plenty who do the space-age thing with elegance and grace. Anyhow, back to history, it has a well-known tendency of repeating itself, and this is especially so when it comes to fashions and styles. The only difference is that they usually return with an added twist that conforms more to the current times.

The next thing I want to express is that by no means is what I am about to share with you to be misconstrued as traits I want you to pick up in attempt to imitate or perpetrate a characteristic fraud. No, I am trying to help you refine and elevate what you are already striving to accomplish, as which of us feel as if we truly do not have our own style? And for the most part I guess I would have to agree that most of you very well may have your own style, only just having a style is not going to cut it. Do you remember the words distinctive, fashionable, elegance, and sophistication? Well, it is these things that set your style apart from that of the average individual's style. Does this mean that you go over and beyond, breaking one's bank or going into debt to stay in all the latest or most expensive fashion, dining in the most luxurious restaurants, or reside in the most lavish living quarters with the most expensive vehicles parked outside? Most certainly not! This would be foolish rather than stylish, but more importantly is the fact that it is not about the price tag on something that makes it stylish or not. Yes, price usually does represent quality, only this is not always the case. The point is this: You actually could take something that was relatively reasonable in pricing, and maybe not even considered to be in style, throw your added twist to it, and what do you know... it's as stylish as ever! Yet this is only because of your characteristic manner and aptitude, or knack of coordinating. The making it your own and owning it after you do so. All the same, if the finer things are within your budget and reasonably so, then why not enjoy them and live to the amplitude of which your situation allows.

With these things covered, we can now move forward to identifying and illustrating the details which you are to pay attention to and work on exercising in order to be able to truly have your own style. Most of these pointers you will be already a bit familiar with, yet for the sake of conveying the message completely for all, I will include them anyhow.

A. Knowing yourself, what you like and what you are comfortable with or in;

B. Gaining a knack for coordinating (colors, designs, styles);

C. Learning to properly present, as presentation is so very important;

D. Be very aware of how you carry yourself at all times, and especially when alone (your etiquette says everything about you);

E. Be very aware of how you speak; very rarely should you have to raise your voice (no matter the situation);

F. Ensure whatever you use to signify your character is not tacky;

G. Maintaining your composure to the best of your ability at all times; and

H. Cease hastiness, and alleviate clumsiness and/or accidents.

With creating and having your own style better understood, we will move on to another directly related issue regarding this subject matter. Understand that I am covering the subtitle here because one is absolutely nothing without the other...

## ALWAYS PROTECT YOUR REPUTATION

Although this subtitle could have been placed anywhere and really should have had its own chapter due to its severe significance, I decided to save it until now and put it in its proper placement. I have done so to emphasize the importance of having your own style and to help you grasp the connection of doing whatever it takes to protect the reputation that you build along the way and with the style you create. Seem a bit tricky? Good, now hang on.

At this stage we have covered a number of related bases, from not to let what others think move you, to not judging others (both of which will be touched on even more throughout the manual). As of now I am sure you're still trying to thread together style and reputation, only do not worry as by the time I have finished, you will know and understand all that there is for you to know and understand.

As I have told you before and will tell you again (in so many ways)... never allow what the next person thinks about you make or break who it is that you are. You know who it is that you are, what you are made of, and what it is that you represent, and truthfully at the end of the day, this is all that matters as you are really the only one who has no other choice but to live with yourself. In addition to that fact, we cannot compel everyone in the world to think highly of us, no matter how hard we try. I mean just think of all of the most noble figures imaginable (both real and mythical) and I guarantee you that none you can think of or research are embraced or highly regarded by ALL. It just goes against the scales of balance that we touched on earlier in this guide. The point is this: If "they" couldn't obtain such a complete clearance of standing... then how could we possibly even begin to think of gaining one?

So now that we have the illusion of being considered or viewed the greatest person in the world out of the way, we can start dealing with the severe significance and clearing up the difference between caring what people's opinions are of you and protecting your reputation. See, the difference is a very simple one. It is one thing for a person to think or feel a certain way about you, what you do, how you do it, or whom you do it with, etcetera. They can think or feel whatever they may, as it's their mind and feelings. The problem (difference) arises when those opinionated or disgruntled individuals decide to voice said opinions or discontentment, or take measures that could or would potentially assassinate your character or reputation. And this is tenfold when said propaganda or actions are slanderous. Clearly the line should no longer be blurred regarding the difference, as to think or feel something and to actually act on these feelings or thoughts are definitely two separate sides of a fence.

An attack on your character/reputation should be taken just as seriously as an attack on your life. Surely we are in agreement that attacks are meant to harm or destroy. In this instance we have something that you put a lifetime of thought, energy, and work into (some even finances) and you have done so because the fact is that your reputation is most times a reflection of your standings within a community (be it yours or someone else's). Now we should also be able to agree that were this a house, building, vehicle, or something you have put your soul into building and someone set out to discredit or destroy it, you would take this extremely personal and take immediate actions to intervene, correct? Well, your character/reputation should be the value of hundreds of these structures to you. It is that one-of-a-kind architecture, your frescos in your Sistine Chapel! So how much more significant can something get?!

The only thing left now is to what extent you are willing to go to protect the reputation that you have built? Of course this is really a question I should be letting you ask and answer for yourself, only since I know for a fact that the end result rests solely with you yourself anyhow, what will my input hurt? So my answer is this: There is absolutely NO extent whatsoever that you should not or would not be willing to go to protect your reputation! Fight fire with fire, eye for an eye, whatever the case may be, there should be no limits. This is you, and everything that you represent and stand for, and under no circumstance should you allow this to be so easily destroyed. So not only are you to contest such with all of your might, but you are to do so wisely, swiftly, determinedly, and as craftily and creatively as possible. That is right—let your battle on behalf of your reputation exhibit the true essence of the character/reputation it is you are protecting in the first place! And most importantly, understand without a doubt that losing can not even begin to be an option. If what you have been building upon is and has been of righteousness, then there is no way that your opposition should succeed in the end. It becomes your duty to best them at every turn. Use your wit, use your charm, and even your aggression when necessary, as when it comes to your reputation... nothing in your arsenal shall be beyond use.

In light of all I have just touched on, I truly hate to give you this last bit of information. Mainly because it's the least of tactics I like to apply, but technically because I will not be giving you a list of other tactics (I am afraid to do so would dull your senses, reflectiveness, and style of combating attacks on your reputation). Anyhow, I must share it with you because not only is it one of the most effective reactions, but even in a worst-case scenario... it gives you time to process everything, plan your best counter, and execute such accordingly. What is this tactic? Silence. A lack of reaction, a lack of acknowledgment, a lack of life to whatever it is your opposition presents. Yet do not forget... this is only for attacks that can be dissolved in such a manner (which should be most). The rest should be fully engaged!

# 9 NEVER BE AFRAID TO STAND ALONE

*You should never be afraid to stand alone,*
*as one day you may very well have to.*
—M.L. Walker Sr.

My motto has, for the longest time, been to never be afraid to be alone. For some reason, early on I realized that any day I could wake up and this be the case, whether by will or fate. A bit drastic, yes maybe; however, it is this motto that conditioned and prepared me for all of the other many ways in which I have found myself abandoned or forced to stand alone. In fact I think this is why in most cases I have always tended to see to whatever affairs of mine on my own, unless I found it absolutely necessary that assistance was required.

There is nothing artful about the quality of being self-reliant. Instead this is based on your will and determination, topped with courage and bravery. You must have the willpower and the determination to stand on what it is that you feel, believe, and represent. You must have the courage and bravery to stand firm when faced with adversity and/or opposition, and not allow yourself to be swayed even when your numbers have dwindled down to just you and yourself (because unfortunately sometimes this may very well end up being the case).

Please do not confuse this quality with a created solitude, as it is far from that. I am in no way suggesting you never accept support, as clearly it could only be a plus to have a constructive support system. What I am trying to explain is that sometimes on your own individual accord or being a representative of something else... you may find yourself being the only one available, functional, usable, or accessible. And if or when these times do come, you as this representative should be fit and prepared, mentally, emotionally, spiritually, and/or physically, to stand in—even if you are forced to do so alone.

Quite naturally there will be times or situations when it is unnecessary, unwise, or outright foolishly insane for you to attempt standing alone. So definitely do not misconstrue this. You do not have to step out there and try to be a lone rider when there truly is no need to be; however, do not be afraid to ride alone if it ever comes to you having to do so. This is all about preparedness. If you are fit and prepared, then when such occasions do happen to arise, you will be more apt to not only deal with but also maneuver said situations.

In all truthfulness it is my most sincere hope that none of you whom this has been created for will ever have to utilize what is covered here in any dire situations. Yet and still, it is extremely wise to instill such not only within yourself but into those closest to you, and especially those you bring into this world or create. I will, however, confess that if the top rung is what you have your sights set on... then you had better get extremely familiar with this quality, as it's almost a requirement to possess such. Ever heard the saying, "It's lonely at the top"? Well, that does not cover exactly what I have attempted to convey here, only it is directly connected and should help me to convey the point. Basically any good follower or leader should never have to worry about being alone, since if you have been being taught right or what you have been teaching is authentic, then the bases should be covered and preparedness on the top of your heads. Speaking of such, we cannot forget the other saying, "heavy is the head," which once again expresses that the likelihood of finding yourself alone in a situation (or maybe even life) is actually a great possibility. Even still, when good or great followers or leaders find themselves in such a position... you won't see them shrink or hide. No, you will see them stand tall with valor and pride... even if they are the last or only one present to stand for the cause! As for the follower, this is the triumph of showing that there is a leader somewhere deep within him or her, and for the leader this is merely a testament of why it is that they are such in the first place!

So remember, whether it is something like standing alone in presenting a fashion statement to standing alone in a dire situation... there is nothing like preparedness and the ability to stand alone if you are forced to. There is nothing in the world like the knowledge, faith, and confidence in yourself that you will never fail yourself! Once you have come to this conclusion, you know that you can be placed anywhere in this world, and as long as it is habitable, you will find a way to not only survive, but thrive!

# 10 BE RESPONSIBLE

*You will be responsible, whether you want to*
*or not. Be it for failure or your success.*
*The choice is yours.*
—M.L. Walker Sr.

Very few of us actually get a kick out of being responsible. This is especially so when growing up. In fact, in our youth we literally shrieked at just the mere thought of such. To take it even further, we make it our business to appear extremely irresponsible, so that when duty is called... we would be the last person to come to mind. Sound familiar? Now let's think about that for a second. Irresponsible = untrustworthy = last person to be called upon. Hmmm...

Clearly this is in direct contrast of the way we will want to be viewed as time goes on. True enough, there may still be certain responsibilities that we would rather be delegated to others as opposed to us, yet the last reason we would want for this to be the case is that we are irresponsible, untrustworthy, and should be the last person called upon. Oh no, any reason but those! So much so that we would even gladly accept the responsibilities that we truly could live without, and do our very best, simply to ensure that no such negative thoughts go through whoever's mind. Why? Contrary to popular belief, it's not to kiss up to them at all (usually, that is—and at least should not be), but rather to make a point or statement that says, "Hey... I can handle any and all responsibilities bestowed upon me." And why is this a point to be made? Because life is full of them. So for each and every responsibility you become accountable for and oversee with finesse or ingenuity... it says that you are qualified to maneuver life's courses and that you can in fact be depended upon if ever needed.

Something else very important about being responsible is that the more responsible you are, the better decisions you make. The better decisions you make, the more in order your life as a whole will be. The more in order your life as a whole is, the less stress you should endure. The less stress you endure, the healthier you will hopefully be. And the healthier you are (as we discussed in Chapter 3), the longer you will hopefully live! See, so something that seems relatively simple in fact has an even more momentous effect than we would ordinarily imagine or give much thought to.

Now the question is, how responsible are you? If the answer is VERY, then that is very good. If anything else... then this is an area in which work is needed and one where there should be no lagging or delays! And do not believe for one second that if you are not responsible by now, then you never will be, because this is absolutely not true. If you truly desire and strive to be responsible, as you should, then there is nothing that can stop you.

The following are some of the things that can be done to help you build confidence in this area and grow more and more responsible with each day.

    A. Lay out a list of things for which you are already responsible or even somewhat responsible;

    B. Start being more attentive to the things you have neglected of your responsibilities, and work harder to fulfill your duties;

    C. Learn the ability to sacrifice so that at times when duty calls and you'd rather play, you will save the play for another day;

D. Do not accept any further responsibilities until you have a complete handle on those which you already have;

E. Once you are in a position whereas you are able to take on extra responsibilities, do not take on anything major. Accept only small or moderate so that you can ensure you get the juggling act down to a science and that if any balls get dropped, it does not stop the show; and

F. When you find yourself being responsible for something, look at this as an honor, and fulfill your responsibility to the fullest of your ability in as timely a fashion as possible.

In addition to duties or personal responsibilities, there are many other little things that actually tie right in and either work for or against your standings. For instance, are you always on time or always late? Are you good with managing your money and usually keep your finance situation in order? Do you pay attention when something important is taking place, or do you utilize that time to talk, text, or joke around? All of these things can help a person decide one way or the other whether you are a responsible individual or not. This does not mean that they will always be correct in their assessment of your level of responsibility, only I must confess that since things of this nature are telltale signs, one would have to take heed to them in order to be safer than sorry. Therefore it is my advice to not only pay keen attention to the details directly involving responsibility, but to also pay just as much attention to those indirect things, because they are all interrelated. So to truly be responsible, you will need to be just as reliable in these areas. Also you should never forget that constantly applying yourself will lead to progress in any areas you are lacking in.

## UNDERSTAND THERE ARE NO SHORTCUTS

Something else that is most important when dealing with being responsible is the fact there are no shortcuts! In life we become so accustomed to finding the easiest or most convenient way to do things and unfortunately we tend to bank on these same devices, implements, and stratagems in the course of our responsibilities being seen to. In all fairness, there is nothing wrong with finding solutions to assist or simplify, as some may at times even increase your level of responsibility. The problem comes in when we attempt to push our responsibility off on these devices, implements, or stratagems as if on some type of auto-pilot or something (kick our feet up while some lullaby app remotely activates when the child you're babysitting starts crying because she is hungry or diaper is wet).

No, there are no shortcuts, and therefore we must not go in looking for them. From my experience it is always best to go in expecting the full brunt of whatever you have found yourself responsible for and to be thankful and appreciative if and when you are fortunate enough to conclude such without as much energy or effort that you may have anticipated. The reason for this is so that you never lose sight of what is truly expected of you and in turn never fail to personally oversee that which you have accepted responsibility for to the best of your knowledge and ability as possible! In all truthfulness, this is truly all that is and can be expected of any of us, as a perfect human being has yet to be created. So in saying this, I am agreeing that no matter if we were the most responsible person on earth... not everything will come off with that appearing to be the case. The thing about it, though, is that as long as you have taken the necessary responsible steps and/or precautions, then it will show—in turn rendering any negative outcomes not being due to irresponsibility. I mean it is no secret that sometimes things just happen, and no matter how responsible we are... we are no match for life!

Still in all, do everything in your power to be as responsible as it will take for you to be viewed, thought of, and remembered as being such. Leave the shortcuts for those who do not take such as seriously as you do. Accept some as they come, if logic agrees that they fit, only you go in with your mind set on standing on whatever it is that you have taken on, because at the end of the day you will be the one who has to own it. That's the main part of being responsible.

# 11 CONTROL YOUR TONGUE

*Words build and destroy, so beware of
those you speak, as once spoken they can
never be taken back.*
—Unknown

I cannot take credit for the quote because although it may be worded in my own way, the basis of the saying is so common that clearly it has been around before my time and conveyed in many different ways. Another one of my favorites is, "Say what you mean and mean what you say." Still in all, what is truly important is the message behind the quotes or sayings. To be completely honest with you, if it were left to me... I would very rarely open my mouth to speak a single word! And yes, I am so very serious. Unfortunately verbal communication is vital to so very many elements of living an active life, and this becomes even more the case when you are living it with the intentions to win.

As expressed in earlier chapters, the controlling of one's tongue is almost impossible for most. Why this is I truly cannot say, and since there are so many different forms of running one's mouth... it would only be safe to say that there are just as many reasons why people cannot help but to do so.

Ironically this makes me think of the old cliché saying, "It's better to be thought the fool than to open your mouth and remove the doubt." What's funny about this is that the vast majority of people do just the opposite as they are so anxious to open their mouths in hopes of proving to everyone else just how smart they are or what all they know. Mind you, the half of them honestly do not be knowing half of what it is they think they do. I mean surely we all have experienced these sort of encounters, time and again. And what about those who will argue with you until blue in the face in attempt to prove their perception is the correct one? Exactly. All humor aside, this subject matter is a very serious one and just so happens to be one of my favorites.

The harsh reality is nobody likes a blabbermouth, as they realize that people who are that long-winded are potentially a risk. For instance, what happens when they no longer have any of their own business to talk about? More times than not, they will begin talking about other people's affairs, and what if they were privy to any of yours? And just to be completely honest with you, the majority of them usually start off with everyone else's before they are forced to confess their own. Another thing is that they spread rumors as truths, like dust particles in the air during a windstorm. Thus making anyone who lacks the ability to harness their tongue a danger to not only themselves but all of those around them. And this is a million times worse now that social media has become such a hit as a sounding board.

On that note I will try to elaborate and break down the core issues by touching on a few directly related areas of this subject. Please take your time to read and understand this very well, as it can and will make all of the difference of the person you are or grow to be.

## NEVER AIR DIRTY LAUNDRY

Personal business, affairs, issues, or concerns of yours and those close to you should NEVER be spoken on or shared with anyone who does not have a vested interest in whatever is being discussed. Nor should sensitive dialogue ever be shared with those who you are well aware are unable to hold water, as we say. In cases whereas they are interested parties, you are to edit what is shared as much as you possibly can, or run the risk of it being the talk of the town or world, depending on your stature, the significance of the information, and the method shared.

Honestly, I could probably give you hundreds of reasons why the sharing of sensitive information should not be shared with outside sources, only I will sum it all up with just two. The first reason is that family issues, as well as that of those closest to you, is and should be treated as being sacred. It is you-all's space and should be respected and protected as such. The second reason is the effect that allowing just anyone to be privy to delicate information can have on those to whom that information means the most, plus your and others' relationships. Nothing can strain a relationship and create conflict like the disclosure of personal information and involvement of parties not invested, and to whom said information is not sacred and will not be protected. And what happens once it finally makes it to the ears of those who do not care much for those whom this sensitive or personal information is most important to?

Your dirty laundry, whether harmless or scandal, is in fact privileged information and therefore you should feel privileged to possess and be the keeper of such. You should view it as your duty to keep this information from the ears and mouths of any and all whom this information should not be entrusted to. And know that you no longer have the excuse of being blind to the facts, as you have been told here and now!

## NEVER ALLOW ALL YOU KNOW TO BE KNOWN

If knowledge is power and the mind a battlefield, then clearly information is the weapon or tool used. Have you ever realized how people are always attempting to pick one another's minds? Surely you have asked yourself sometimes why it is that one person would even want to know some of the things they appear interested in knowing, as it was truly of no substance or significance. The reason for this is because what appears to be nothing much to you happens to be just a step closer to everything to the next person. Look at it as a mental game of chess. Exactly, I can just about imagine the thoughts going through your mind and feeling that just coursed down your spine. However, to answer the question of why exactly they would want to know certain things or better yet, what's at stake, I can tell you that sometimes it could be absolutely nothing more than the knowledge of knowing they have the most vital pieces on the board. Yet you have to assume that it is everything, because if things ever were to go south... this is what they have prepared for and thus the reason why the knowledge obtained produces a level of comfort as to a position of power.

The following is a number of things to keep in mind and continuously exercise in your daily life, in hopes of aiding you to not give so freely of that which can and will be used against you, and not just in a court of law.

    A. Be extremely cautious of who all you allow inside your mind, as not everyone is worthy of this access;

    B. Be extremely selective of what all you disclose, when and how you do so. All of these factors are crucial;

    C. A rule of thumb is that if an individual or group has no vested interest in information, then clearly it is none of their business and should NOT be shared. It serves absolutely no purpose and can only do more harm than good to involve them;

    D. For those who are involved and do have a vested interest, the information shared should not exceed that which is absolutely necessary to satisfy their requirement of their knowledge to assist in their fulfilling functions;

    E. Learn to sort through data or information in your mind, establishing what can be put into play and most importantly... what is off limits from being put into play;

F.  Understand that sometimes misinformation or misdirection is necessary; and

G.  Be meticulous about remembering who you tell what, to lessen any mystery surrounding leaks.

All of us have heard the "think before you speak" bit before (too many times to count, right?). Well, not only is this so true, it is an understatement. I personally could not emphasize it enough. In short, not only should you stop and think before you open your mouth and speak, you should stop and think two, three, and maybe even four times. Before you actually let words spill out, ask yourself what exactly are you about to say, how are you going to say it, and are the ears that are about to receive the words deserving or creditable enough to receive what it is that you are about to convey. Even when small talking and/or misdirecting... your words possess power. Yes, I know that to most of you this may come as a surprise, yet it is the truth. And just to prove it to you, I will give you the prime example and allow you to visualize all of the many possibilities from there. See, what it boils down to is the fact that as long as there is one person who believes in you and the words that you speak, then at the very least your words hold power with that one person. Correct? Now... let's imagine that person has at least one person who believes in their word and they pass your words along, and so on and so on. We see it all day every day, and with some of the most ridiculous things. Yet all it takes is for it to be received for it to be perceived and then believed. Therefore is not this more than enough evidence that even your voice has the power to spread?

## SECRETS ARE ONLY THAT IF KEPT

Surely I do not need to tell you the significance of secrets or keeping them. I mean clearly we all know what they are as well as why they exist. I too agree that nobody likes them outside of those whose secrets are to be kept, yet I must also agree that some things are better off taken to the graves of those to whom they belong. Though I can assure you that the masses would much rather they be revealed, no matter what damage they may leave in their wake and/or to whom.

Now as much as I would truly love to instill in you the ability to keep a secret, the fact remains that either you can or cannot, or will or will not be able to keep a secret. What I would like for you to give a thought to is this... what if the secret was yours? Well, let me rephrase that, because for some strange reason we all tend to feel that at least one other person must know even ours (which is a fallacy). Therefore I will say, what if it were a secret of yours that if ever revealed would undoubtedly destroy you?! Yes, that's more like it. Sit and ponder that for a while. And while you are at it, give thought to what would be the reaction of a person whose secret of such magnitude you were the beholder of and they felt such had been betrayed!

# 12 MASTER YOUR SURROUNDINGS

*Get to know your surroundings like you
know yourself, as this will help you
maneuver them with finesse.*
—M.L. Walker Sr.

As crazy as this may sound, I am a firm believer that our surroundings are conversationalists that are always eager to give us the deep dark secrets integrated within its every crease and crevice. And why should I care about what is going on around me or what is all around me, if I am not a part of it or it does not affect me directly, you ask? At which point I say, you know what... you are right, that's the end of this chapter. Of course I am just kidding. The fact is that knowing your surroundings is primarily a key survival tactic; however, it also serves many more purposes, with most revolving around giving you different options and advantages. Also it must be noted that surroundings in this context includes, but is not limited to, where it is you reside. Basically it could be places that you frequent regularly or are simply visiting for the first, and last, time. It can also be the people or situations you find yourself surrounded by or in.

## LISTEN CAREFULLY AND PAY CLOSE ATTENTION

Let's take a look at the blind. Now surely none of us would want to be as unfortunate to lose our sight, just as it would be safe to say that the majority of those with this disability would love to simply be able to see. Still in all, let's look at the facts. Those who have lost their sight gained a different vision. They tap into a sense or a real awareness and many of them take this far beyond the confines of their homes. My theory is that they create these sort of maps in their minds, and pay keen attention to the smallest of details, such as the smell of cake that lets them know they are passing the bakery at the corner of their block, or maybe the bump in the road that lets them know their stop is coming up on the local bus route.

I guess what I am asking you is for you to get more in tune with the inner blind side of yourself, and to put all of your other senses to work a little more than you normally would. Really I should say to simply pay more attention to your senses than you usually do, because our senses are usually hard at work most times anyhow; however, we tend to disregard most of what they register and attempt to relay as being unimportant. To be sure you understand exactly what I am attempting to convey here, I will give you some prime examples that will hopefully guide you in the right direction. Some may be a bit familiar to you already, and others may be a little drastic, only it is my job to drive home the correlation.

    A.  The squeaking of a step or door in your home, as this gives you a sense of position of person(s) who may or may not supposed to be there or in those places;

    B.  Outdoor lighting, from being on and off to the different reflections they give off when obstructed for whatever reason, since this aids your ability to be vigilantly aware (what if someone is standing on your porch without knocking or ringing the doorbell, or maybe a porch light that is usually on is all of a sudden off, yet you know it's only a month old);

C. Your neighbor's dog's behavior or barking patterns, because if it's acting as it does when the children are out back in the daytime at half past midnight, then chances are something's not quite right;

D. Traffic or neighborhood activity at certain times of day or night. These things are usually pretty consistent in most neighborhoods and an unknown vehicle out of place could very well mean more than what meets the eye;

E. A lot of cities, businesses, and homeowners are utilizing video surveillance now that technology has made such more feasible. So although it would be good to know where each of these were, this would be impossible, due to such inconspicuous devices and placement. And the fact that even cellphones now have the ability to record. Therefore as expressed in other chapters, it would be best if you just simply assumed that at any given moment of any day you are being watched, and therefore what would it hurt for you to be just as aware?

Surely to some of you this may seem a bit excessive; however, I would like to point out one thing. These things as well as the many other that you will think of do not require you to approach in an excessive manner. The fact is that you can subtly approach these matters with no other intentions but to make mental notes (create the maps as the blind do), and after consistently doing so, your senses will naturally adapt and grow stronger in regards to registering these things so that if and when the time comes that something is not as it should be... your instincts of acute awareness (spidey senses) should automatically kick in and take over.

Now to touch more on what we all first think of when we are told to listen. Something about me is the fact that I will listen to even a baby for a second if it is trying to talk. I know you are thinking, "Well, that's silly, we all do that." I would agree we all do so to a certain extent. The difference is that when these same children or others get to an age where they are truly able to speak, most people are no longer patient enough to lend that same ear. True enough their young minds are very imaginative; however, what happens that one time when they are trying to tell you about that man on the side of your house in a mask with a gun? See how quickly that just got very serious now that it is coming from me? Would it have gotten as serious had it been coming from the child? The fact is that warnings come in many different forms and can come from the young, elderly, or the signs of your surroundings alike. It's all on you as to whether or not you will be attentive enough to take heed.

## LEARN THE ART OF READING SITUATIONS

It is one thing to have a map of indicators embedded in your mind, but it is completely another to be able to use these indicators to read the situations for which they have been memorized, in order to help you avoid said perils. Therefore if creating the maps of indicators is the Yin, then conditioning yourself to take notice of your inner voice (mental alarms, or whatever you would like to call it) would have to be the Yang. See, the two go hand in glove and it is your job to ensure that it is an appropriate fit. Meaning you need to take the mere seconds out of your days to condition your mind for an easy transition of mapped-out indicators, to taking heed to them and subsequently acting upon such to protect yourself and/or those close to you, in case danger is in fact lurking.

It would be impossible for me to foresee the future or what exactly your actions should be in order to avoid becoming a victim of circumstances. Yet and still, I will attempt to give you a few examples to try and help you understand exactly what is I am explaining. Once again some of these examples may already be familiar to you; however, others may not. Nonetheless I only hope to open your eyes and mind, because sometimes these perils may go beyond what you have mapped out, yet alarms will still go off.

A. You enter a setting unfamiliar to you that has others in attendance who you also are unfamiliar with. It is your job to get a feel for the energy, verbal and non-verbal cues;

B. You are somewhere you are familiar with and surrounded by people you are familiar with, yet some or all are acting different. You may want to vacate the scene or at least inform those closest to you to be focused in case you all need to make a quick exit;

C. When driving, you must pay close attention to whether you are being followed or the feel for your surrounding once halted at stop signs or red lights. I personally made a habit of utilizing all mirrors when driving and controlled the passenger mirror when I was only a passenger;

D. When pulling up to stores or locations, you should always try to quickly assess the situation, because most times when something does not feel right, something usually is not;

E. When people ask you to do things that you know is odd of them to ask you. Be it out of character for them or you, pay very close attention and take heed;

F. When people you never have any dealings with try to attach themselves to you for whatever reason... BEWARE! In fact in this day and age, you should be cautious of meeting new people period (see later chapters).

These are just a handful to help give you an idea; however, life and situations are constantly changing and therefore it is more-so the art of having a feel for gauging or feeling them out that I am more concerned with. It is my belief that once you become in tune with these aspects and apply them with others, such as "Being Adaptable" to the ever-evolving situations and surroundings, that you will be better suited to maneuver them. Not to mention how amazingly great you will feel once you begin reading situations far enough ahead that you are able to remove yourself from the equations and unworthy people from your life, prior to it becoming costly to you in any shape, form, or fashion. So this is why early assessments are necessary, because it's usually those who obtain and retain the advantage that end up winning! And no... do not allow this ability to be confused with being paranoid. Finesse it and the difference will be evident.

# 13 KNOW HOW TO DIFFERENTIATE

*Sometimes knowing the difference is the*
*difference that makes all the difference.*
—M.L. Walker Sr.

Being able to differentiate the difference between people
and things you involve yourself with will prove to be one of
the most important things you may ever set your sights on
accomplishing. So often we as human beings misconstrue the
extent of relationships, nature of situations, or our positions in
different circumstances. This is a flaw that will cost you more
than it will ever earn you, and as you maneuver this chapter
and begin to reflect and compare... you will clearly see where
you have already come up short time and time again due to not
distinguishing the differences that were so obvious that you
should have many times over.

There are a number of aspects related to this chapter, and
being that this is something close to me, I feel these different
aspects deserve their own categories, so that specific attention
can be given to each one. For the most part I feel as if the facts
will be self-explanatory and therefore I will not stress the
importance of taking heed. What I will stress is how you
should accept the facts for what they are worth and try to

refrain from justifying acceptance of the results you failed to acknowledge and prevent. Now we proceed....

## BETWEEN FAMILY AND RELATIVES

Let's get one thing straight for those of you who may not understand that just because you and someone else may share the same blood or lineage DOES NOT make you and them family! A relative, most definitely, but the truth is that sometimes people you share absolutely no ancestral lineage with can be more of a family member to you than those you are directly related to. Yes, as impossible as this may seem, it is very true. I will admit that it may not happen the extent whereas we could count it as more frequent than actual family bonding, yet it is still common enough that it should not be overlooked.

The issue here is that like with love, family is an action word. It is something that is evident as it is constantly being done and shown. In my eyes it's all about love, honor, respect, and support. So if a person who is related to you is failing in any of these areas, then you may want to stop and do a little evaluating. And this is especially so if those individuals are constantly displaying the direct opposite, because if a person is never failing to show you that they do not love, honor, respect, or support you... then clearly what elements of DNA you all share means absolutely nothing to them! So if it means absolutely nothing to them, then why in the hell should it mean much of anything to you? Does this mean they are your enemy or that you should go out of your way to make them such? Not at all. Most importantly, you should never make unnecessary enemies (which will be discussed further in later chapters), but being that they are still your relative and are or may be more like family to those who are family to you, you should at the very least respect that. Yet and still, recognize and know the difference so that you treat them no more like family than they do you. If they are cordial, then you should be as well. If they are distant, then respect their desire to be so. Sure it's okay to try to mend gaps; however, you should not waste too much of your time or energy on such if, after a few attempts, they have made it clear where exactly it is they stand. Also their reasoning really should not have too much importance to you, as there is no grey area whereas being family is concerned (we accept and appreciate regardless of flaws and/or shortcomings and expect the same in return).

Now you may have noticed that I did not include trust in the equation. My reason for this is because for the most part, it's obvious that we do and will always trust our family before anyone else. The other reason is that even with family, there are certain things we will or will not trust them with. There are too many different aspects of this and way too many reasons why we will or will not, which range from relevant to irrelevant, yet none of them play a factor in whether or not we know, without a shadow of a doubt, that they are truly our family members and are there for us just as much as we are there for them!

As expressed earlier, we cannot forget the unexpected family bond and ties. Be it cousins like siblings, relatives of mates, in-laws, or simply friends who fit more as a family unit. We must be thankful and show our gratitude for such blessings. The reality is that sometimes some people just feel more at home or more in sync with others, and since we all are the human race, it is extremely possible for certain people to be naturally in tune with one another more than those we would assume they should more than likely be in tune with. Why exactly this is could be theorized many times over, only the truth is that it really does not even matter. It's a factual possibility and we should all hope to be as blessed to have that adopted family or member, just for those times that our relatives fail to live up to the standards of being considered family.

In closing on this aspect, I have to share with you just one of many examples (as my family has become family to a number of people who were not born into it). While growing up, my grandmother, although not racist but definitely skeptical of white people, had a little pudgy friend named Maxine

Creyts. To this day I have no idea where Maxine was actually from or how they even met, only I know it had to be a sight to see this little white woman popping up over to this house full of black people every single day. She did not drive and only lived around the corner, so she would walk around there and spend her days with what grew to be her family. I remember times where we would have to go around there and check up on her if she had not showed or to help her with things around her house, and for those of us assigned to do so there was never a complaint, as she was one of ours. If she had any other family I do not know; however, what I do know is that her remaining days of laughter, pain, or sorrow were spent and shared with the family she had grown a part of, and that years later, once she finally departed this earth... I was truly saddened and heartbroken, because I knew without a doubt that we had lost a piece of our family. No, she did not speak or act like us but none of that mattered, because she knew how to love, honor, respect, and be supportive like us, and we accepted her as she came.

## BETWEEN FRIENDS AND ASSOCIATES

For starters it is my opinion that true friends are hard to find, and therefore every friendly encounter should not be approached with the anticipation that it will result in a sincere friendship. Still, our lives consist (usually) of constantly meeting new people, with a nice portion of them actually appearing to be decent people that we really would not have no problem with allowing into our lives, and most times we do. The question is how many of these turn out to actually become friends as opposed to associates? Actually I guess we would first have to establish what your definition of a friend is. My definition of a friend is something close to what I expressed to you regarding family, only I also do believe that time, space, and circumstances can at times have adverse effects on friendships. However, it should be made clear that if it does not last longer than twelve months, then that was not really much of a friendship at all, but rather more of an association

THE UNIVERSAL GUIDE TO LIFE

(as close as some may be), and just because it does last longer does not necessarily make it more, just increases the likelihood that it is or was.

From my experience, being able to differentiate the difference between a friend and associate was not initially as easy as we would like to think it would be. The reason for this is the fact that most associates have learned to mimic all the true qualities and traits of a friend, and will do so as long as you serve the purpose of the association. Unfortunately you, under the illusion of friendship, are not always made aware of the purpose of the association, and therefore are unable to know when it has run its course. Then again not all associations are severed quickly upon purposes being served, and this is usually because your associates figure why not stay loosely associated since they never know if or when you may be needed to serve additional purposes.

True friendship, on the other hand, does not require much of anything but the love, respect, honor, trust, and support of a person you have allowed the privilege of being one of the closest individuals to you in the whole world and vice versa. There are no unseen motives or no purpose other than hopefully sharing a lifelong friendship. So yes, this does leave us in a peculiar position, because we do not want to close off or treat every situation we are presented with to make a new friend as merely an associate-making opportunity. Yet and still we are to approach these situations from a realistic point of view. And just for the record, I am not in any way suggesting that it is impossible for associates to become friends, only I am suggesting that you should enter these situations being able to differentiate the difference between the two, because once a person's mind is made up that you are nothing more than an associate... that is usually about all that you will ever be to them, regardless of what you may perceive the relationship to be. And with this being the case, why should you go out of your way to try and make it more than what it is or will ever be? I will clarify one thing, though: If you and the other person both came into the situation with a common goal or purpose in mind, then yes, the potential for future friendship could very well exist. The problem comes in when and where the connection is one-sided, as opposed to there being a precise understanding you are being misled or misused. Other than that, having an associate is not necessarily a bad thing, since at times we too need people to serve different purposes in our lives, that those closest to us cannot or are just not fit to do so from your perspective. Basically it is all about getting your fair share out of the relationship.

I will now give you a few examples to help further penetrate your mind and help you pinpoint some of the telltale signs of a potential friend or associate. This one will be a little different: as opposed to me telling you what each is, I will give the example and leave it on you to decide what each one could potentially be to you.

A. This person never calls unless there is a catch to them doing so;

B. This person calls you most times to see how you are doing and feeling;

C. This person comes by sometimes to pick you up and just hang out;

D. This person only comes to hang out with you when they have something they would like for you to do with or for them;

E. This person never really shares personal information regarding their life, but always asks you about yours;

F. This person usually gives just as much as they take in the relationship; and

G. This person sees you at an event and simply waves instead of actually acknowledging you or catching up.

Clearly I could go on for days with this, only hopefully you get the picture and are able to start creating your own list of examples to assist you with differentiating the difference, as there is no reason you should allow yourself to come up short in the relationships you build with people who intend merely to utilize you as a stepping stone. Of course with sincere friendships things like that are not even of a concern, but this is why you need to know, so that you do not give so much of yourself for less than nothing in return.

## THE GAME AND THE STREETS

As truth would have it, this is one aspect I would have liked to leave out of this manual; however, for me to do so would have left this incomplete. The fact is that the game and the streets both play a very important part of life, no matter what side of the fence you are on, if for no other reason than the domino effects that make it easier for those on the other side to turn right back around and affect the game or streets directly (which is an entirely different story). In all honesty, what most consider as the game I consider the "Game Of Life" because it covers so much terrain, and at the end of the day the goal is as common as could possibly be. And the streets... oh, the streets are real, no cut no chaser!

I will start with the "game." Contrary to belief, the game is more than just drugs or crime. Nor is it the "easy way out," as most would try to make it. Yes, some may unnecessarily take this route under the pretenses of it being easier; however, once all is said and done, I am sure that even they themselves would have to admit that it is anything but easy. Now to be a little bit more specific, the "game" is what the masses associate with criminal activity. I personally view it as when people find loopholes and do their best to exploit them. And before you frown your nose, first think about the fact that most crimes did not and do not actually become criminal until the powers that be or those close to them have had their run and decide it is time to turn the faucets off to keep others from following suit, at which time the particular avenues of making money have laws enacted or harsher penalties implemented. And although I will not throw names out there... do your research on the most hated or loved presidents, their families, and their business associates. And that will give you a nice start on understanding what I am saying (and no, I am not talking about President Obama). My point is go back and take a look at how some of these individuals and corporations built their wealth and the things that took place afterwards to prevent others from doing the same, while allowing the truly corrupt to maintain and monopolize theirs.

The "game" is about knowing what most people do not regarding different routes to acquiring finances in different markets and/or arenas, and being able to effectively exploit such directly or indirectly (hence the old saying, "game is to be sold, not told"). In fact this very guide could be considered "game" as some of the very tactics within are specifically designed to aid you in maneuvering and coming out ahead of the pack in pretty much any market or arena you see fit to venture into. And for those that it was created for, your loyalty to the movement is your payment (so don't fall short). Anyhow, what this says is that "game" does not remove the pretext of value, as true value can be found in many different forms. Got it?

Now we will move along to the "streets." Make no mistake about it, the streets are grim and if you have allowed yourself to think or believe anything different, then you are sadly mistaken! When people talk about playing or being in the streets, they are referring to frequenting areas that are usually ripe with criminal elements. Most would call these areas the ghetto, hood, slum, or urban areas, only at the end of the day when we speak of people in connection with the streets, it is usually those who, at any given time, can be found there, or at the very least will pop up daily and more than likely several times throughout the day. The fact is that the "streets" is more a lifestyle and, despite the popular belief of the masses, everyone who lives in these neighborhood or areas is not actually a part of it. Yes, they may have more of a free rein, only what would those misinformed expect... they live there!

So there we have the difference between the "game" and "streets," and the reason why it is important for you to differentiate the difference between the two is because although I would never advise or suggest that you disregard being on top of your "game" while being fortunate enough to play this game called life... I would strongly advise against playing the "streets." Why? Because first and foremost, the streets are not for everyone. In fact very few are actually built for that lifestyle, which tends to be very harsh and gruesome. For those who have been directly influenced by the lifestyle but have not succumbed to it, you should consider yourself blessed, since you now have a gift of a lot of what has and will be covered in this guide and therefore it would be safe to say that your adapting and survival in these type of environments would be greater than those who have not. The bottom line is that the life expectancy of those dedicated to the streets is far less than pretty much any other lifestyle, and this is including the Armed Forces. So you absolutely do not have to play the streets in order for you to play the game, and if you plan on winning the "game," then know that it will not be done in the streets (no matter how good you can become at it). Be wise and work to finesse your understanding and acquiring of "game."

# 14 LEARN FROM YOUR AND OTHERS' MISTAKES

*Mistakes are counterproductive and costly,*
*so you should never want to make*
*the same one twice.*
—M.L. Walker Sr.

Here I once again admit that not a single one of us is perfect, and therefore it would be literally impossible for any of us to avoid making mistakes altogether. Why mistakes are unavoidable is not much of a mystery at all, just as your curiosity surrounding such isn't. The fact is that life is made up of trial-and-error moments, and it is very rare that we get things absolutely correct the very first time around. This is why mistakes are such a common occurrence, and although some of the previous and following chapters will try to help you create preventive habits in attempt to avoid potential mistakes... this chapter will deal predominantly with quickly identifying mistakes made and learning how not to make the same ones again and again.

If there was one main area I would want to start by drawing attention to, it would have to be the denial phase that we first go through. Trust me, I understand very well how our minds, for some odd reason, cause us to believe that if we continue to think or tell ourselves "that didn't happen like that" or "there has to be a mix-up, maybe I am just tripping," the end results will somehow change what they already are. Well, as I am sure you all are fully aware, it will not! Tomorrow the facts will remain. So why is this part such a big issue? Because sometimes timing is everything, and by skipping the denial phase you could move straight to the search for resolution phase, and possibly avoid making the same mistake immediately or compounding the one already made.

So yes, obviously identifying that a mistake has been made, and what exactly the mistake consisted of would have to be your main focus. The only way for this to even begin to take place is and will be for you to accept them for what they are and refrain from trying to psych yourself out and make it be something other than what it actually is. Once over these hurdles, you will then be able to focus more on how said mistakes were even made in the first place. It is my belief that identifying these factors are very crucial because it is only then that you would be able to properly process this information so that you could then program yourself with the necessary preventive techniques and measures.

Are your mistakes the only ones you can learn from? Of course not. In most cases you will learn that you actually can and will learn more from others' mistakes than you will your own. Why? Because clearly you are only one person, and even if you were the most mishap-ed person on this earth... there is still only so many mistakes you could possibly make in a lifetime. Yet with there being more people around you, chances are you will be more likely to witness or hear about mistakes being made daily, and in some cases even get the full details so that you can fully analyze the situations from front to back. You should never fail to take full advantage of such a privilege, and this is especially so whereas it involves an area in which you are involved or may one day become so involved in.

The bottom line is that only a fool would be okay with or constantly want to make mistakes. Yes, living life consists of making them, and there will never be a foolproof way of preventing them from ever being made, yet we being a people striving to know, do, and be better... making mistakes would be in direct contrast to this.

There are two things that are common factors of preventive measures, and they are your natural instincts (also considered your intuition), as well as being forewarned by others. These actually could help you before said mistakes are even made in the first place. And yes, I know very well how we, for some strange reason, refuse to listen or pay attention to either, only if we claim to have any sense at all... then we will begin to start doing so, as much as we possibly can. Oh, I agree that solutions of other people are not always accurate or precisely on point. Still, it could not hurt much to, at the very least, take heed to the forewarning, as well as trying to remain conscious of such when and where they would apply.

# 15 LEARN THE ART OF READING PEOPLE

*People are like books: every aspect of us*
*holds or helps propel a story or lesson*
*that should be studied.*
—M.L. Walker Sr.

Unless you have spent the majority of your life sheltered from the rest of the world, you have heard the saying, "People are creatures of habit." Well, this could not be more true, and the older (sometimes wiser) we get, it becomes more evident. Amazingly we witness this throughout our entire lives, at times even taking note of such, but very rarely do we process the true significance of fully understanding the psychology of mankind. Yes, we all at some point tend to make a meager attempt at doing so, yet it usually takes for our alert systems to be activated, giving rise to extra awareness. Of course there are those who are simply self-conscious or maybe even borderline paranoid schizophrenic, and although they apply a form of studying the mental and behavioral characteristics of others... it is so overt that even those as inept as they themselves are able to pick up on the vibe, subsequently making adjustments so as to keep themselves in check as much as possible. Now imagine this same scenario with a masterful adapter on the opposite side. Surely someone is going to be at a great disadvantage.

I am sure that the first thought to come to the majority of you guys' minds after reading this chapter's title was the books they have on body language. The fact is that even though these subjects are directly related and you cannot have one without the other, what we are dealing with here is slightly different. As you will see, we will be focusing more on the mental aspect rather than the physical. Yes, some physical will be touched on; however, so much in regards to the physical is covered by common sense that I figure we would get straight to the core, which actually controls it all.

## DIRECT OBSERVATION

Sometimes it is okay to stare directly at a person. Usually you are already familiar with this person, acquainted in some fashion or newly introduced with the notion of future encounters. We usually observe their appearance and then their mannerism; however, the good part is when you are able to stare them directly in the eyes. Yes, I too agree that it is not polite to stare, howbeit short intervals shall excuse you of distastefulness. And just as a pointer, it is easier to stare someone in the eyes when you are actually speaking with them. Back to the subject at hand, the reason staring into the eyes is best is because when you do so, most people will automatically begin inadvertently telling you things about themselves (hence the "windows to the soul"), as well as others.

Yes, a lot of this will be verbal, more than likely not all will be true, nevertheless you will be given all of the dots to connect. It is on you to know and be able to recognize the signs. Maybe their voices crackle at certain points, they begin to stutter, or that southern accent subtly disappears. Plus we always have the physical, which so many of us are so dependent on already (shifting of the eyes, hands, feet-jitters). The thing is to be able to pinpoint and pull out the indicators (which we will cover more later on in this chapter), so that you can sort and file them in your memory bank for later, or sometimes immediate, evaluation.

## INDIRECT OBSERVATION

The fact is that even with direct observation it is not best to always allow a person to actually "know" that they are being "read." In the case of indirect observing, the very last thing you want is for your person of interest to be aware of your intent to get a read on them. Of course this will not be successful all of the time; however, no matter the case, when using this method you are to be as less intrusive as possible.

Whereas it is most times the intensity of the direct observation that drives the person being observed to give off the signs to be read, with the indirect observing it is subtlety that creates the mental imbalance that subsequently drives the observed into giving off signs. Just reflect back on the many times your sensors have been triggered and the alarm has gone off in your mind, telling you that someone had their eyes on you or were attempting to get a reading on you. We usually do the first thing that comes to mind and try to locate the source. Yes, sometimes we just continue; nevertheless we become alert and immediately begin our scan.

There is something else very interesting that takes place once we become conscious of a possible observation. Without hesitation or delay our thought process switches to adjusting and correcting any and everything that we even suspect is out of order or place. It is at this very moment that we begin to give the necessary signs for our potential observers to start their reading. If we have singled out who exactly it is and evaluated their importance or lack thereof, we will decide whether or not we proceed with the corrective actions and/or to what extent.

Sometimes we will remain uncertain, as if someone is peering through shades of their glasses or tint of their windows (techniques commonly used), it becomes a bit complicated ascertaining whether or not you are correct in your suspicions. Other times the observer may simply be a curious spectator or even lost in a trance daydreaming, yet we still take heed to the sensors and continue to give way to the indicators (consciously, subconsciously, blatant, or subtle), which subsequently lead to us giving off the signs to be read.

## INDICATORS

As mentioned above, indicators play a pivotal role in learning to read people, be it direct or indirect observation. True enough it may take you some time to become fully in tune with the indicators; however, since the majority of them are physical, you should already have a slight idea of what some of them are, just never really knew the significance or maybe even mistook them as the signs. I will do my best to try enlightening you all to the differences between the indicators and actual signs, only the reality is that if you can simply get a grasp of the signs, know how to categorize them and what traits to attach to them... this may suffice.

Before I proceed with examples, let it be noted that the main reason this is such a task is because most of the indicators and signs are things that people do every day, all day long, while at the very same time it is that reason which makes it achievable. Remember when I began this chapter, I did so by touching on us being creatures of habit, so with this being the case, the task then becomes to be able to distinguish when such is a natural action or a provoked reaction. The harsh reality is that for even those who acquire an in-depth understanding and advanced ability to read others, you can never do so successfully a hundred percent. The fact is you will be lucky to get sixty out of that and great to get seventy-five. Why? Because the difference is so slight that misreading indicators and/or signs at times can be a common occurrence, and this is why this chapter was not titled "Master The Art Of Reading People." And with this out of the way, we will get to a few examples.

> A. You are attempting a direct observation read, beginning with a simple handshake or greeting after introduction. Most people on the opposite

end will proceed cautiously, as not only do they not know you but they too are attempting to get a read on you. However, if they are overly nervous or fidgety, this more than likely is an indicator, at which time one should ease off and switch to indirect observation;

B. You are applying the indirect reading and during such, the person being read is constantly attempting to catch you in the act. This could easily be considered an indicator this person is jittery when in fact more than likely they just have a keen sense of perception;

C. You are attempting a direct observation reading and the person being read, instead of trying to inconspicuously address anything that may be out of place with himself or herself, asks you, "Is anything in my nose?" or "Does this fit me correctly?" Something as simple as whether they do so with or without contact could be the indicator of which category you would start your database, yet regardless of that, you must not overlook the indicator that your study may be transparent and easy to read. Then again they may already know for a fact and are merely preparing for a counter-read by loosening your spine to peel your covers back flat.

As you can see, the core of any read is being able to decipher the differences of vague and the subtlest of actions. The beauty of this is that for whose of you who are able to tap into this ability, you will know without a doubt when you have done so and as you get better at it. Fortunately for you all, there is now social media and its news feeds to assist you considerably. Yet and still, even that advantage will never compare to the hands-on practice that will eventually become as natural as breathing is to you. This is unless you are or aim to be a recluse.

## COUNTERING READS

To be honest with you, the best way to counter reading others attempt on you is to simply be comfortable in your skin, and confident in a number of the other chapters covered in this manual. When that is the case, then you will have full control of the signs you allow to go out for others to read and thus the potential readers will only have what it is you give them to read or go off of.

As you become more in tune with the reading of others and the many different signs they give off for you to catalog and evaluate, you will become just as in tune as to what you should not do to keep from giving off signs of your own.

I would like to hope that there was or is no reason for me to explain why it is that you would want or need to read people or what exactly it is that you are looking to learn by doing so. Anyhow, if these are things that you are unsure of, just continue to read and learn from this guide and it will eventually become so crystal clear to you why this is necessary to aid you in maneuvering life's course.

# 16 CHOOSE YOUR PARTNERS CAREFULLY

*Man is the only animal that can remain on friendly terms with the victims he intends to eat, until he eats them.*

—Samuel Butler

Throughout our lives, most of us will take on many different types of partners, for many different things, at many different stages and for many different reasons. Some of these partners will serve their purpose and prove to be worth their weight in gold. Others will prove to be pretty much useless and a waste of time, energy, and possibly finances. Then of course there will be those who will attempt to remove your having a choice in the matter altogether, by simply throwing themselves into your life and acting as if that is their rightful place in this world.

In "Choose Your Partners Carefully," we must first understand that this refers to all different types of relationships and/or every different level of them. Chiefly this deals with *knowing* who exactly it is that you are dealing with! Don't just assume that you know all there is to know about someone you associate with. Make it a priority to get to know that person as completely as you possibly can.

Within every relationship you have, be it intimate, business, criminal, or whatever it may be... there should or must be a courting process. I know to many of you this may sound dated or maybe a bit excessive, but look at it from this point of view: In the word courting is the root word *court*! Whenever matters are brought before a court, both sides attempt to present and discredit things presented as facts, all in hopes of revealing the truth, so that a decision or judgement can be rendered. These facts must first be discovered in order for any of this to take place, and this is called the *discovery* process, which is the gathering of all relevant information, evidence, and facts possible prior to entering a courtroom and attempting to try or defend a case. And without it there is no proceeding. Make sense? Well, this is the same process that must be exercised when courting potential partners. We should, or rather must, try to discover as much about those we deal with as we can, before we make such decisions as inviting them into our personal space, onto our teams, into our homes, make part of our businesses, or just into our lives, period!

Yes, it is true that some things may only be revealed in the midst of trials and tribulations. We cannot get around this fact, as some people wear their masks extremely well, and/or are astute in the art of deception. However, it is very possible that by being diligent in our research, observation, and studying of these individuals in their dealings with us and others, we will, at the very least, gather enough knowledge of them to enlighten us as to what we could or should rationally be able to expect during the trials and/or tribulations. No, we can never know for certain, and as you may already know or will soon learn, people are good at surprising one another where our expectations of one another is concerned! Yet this is why the minimizing of these surprises is what we are aiming to do here. Well, at least the negative ones, because it actually works both ways in some people's eyes. I personally do not feel a person should be surprised or even consider it a surprise when someone does just what it is they should, are supposed to, or are expected to do. Still, there was no better way for me to make the desired point.

I am now going to shift a little in order to further explain just what it is that you should be paying attention to and seeking out of these potential partners. So follow me closely on this. As expressed in "Create Balance In Your Life," the nature of man/woman is dual, one side being animality and the other divinity. Without both, none of us could be complete. It is the sinister animalistic traits that we are to be most concerned with sniffing out, as these are the traits most of us tend to want to suppress or keep concealed, and usually will go to just about any extent to achieve the latter. For most, scriptures is the best source of obtaining accounts of man and his duality; however, for others such as myself, living day to day is the best teacher of these lessons. Sometimes it is easy to determine who we are dealing with simply by knowing ourselves and mastering ourselves. But regardless of any of this... people will *always* show you exactly who they are. You just have to remove the blinders and be willing to see them from an unbiased point of view.

Luckily for you, all technology and science has become so advanced that it gives you an advantage that those of my day simply did not have. Am I suggesting that you accept everything you discover through search engines or social media sites as accurate? Not at all, since not everything that will be seen or found via these sources will always be a hundred percent correct. What I am suggesting, though, is that you not be afraid to utilize resources of this nature, because you cannot afford to take the purpose of this chapter for granted by continuing to accept individuals' credence off of word of mouth, self-certification, or "face value" alone. Reflect on past predicaments you or those closest to you have found yourself in, or those you've witnessed firsthand. Clearly the worst happens way too often, and therefore it is solely your responsibility to do the necessary research to discover who the individuals you are now or may end up dealing with actually are. Believe it or not, most people are savages who have lost all knowledge of their true self and are now living beastly lives where the smart prey on the strong, the strong prey on the weak, and the weak prey on the young or dumb. So protect yourself by knowing those you get involved with, or you just might suffer from a plague. Tap into your divine side and you will realize not only how to avoid being anyone's prey, but how to govern all of the above-mentioned predators.

There are a number of ways to get an idea of whether a person is upright or if that person has indeed fallen. A few of them are as follow:

A. Concluding by inference or evidence;
B. Fore-knowledge and experience;
C. Human nature; and
D. Your inner voice.

As with everything else that comes with making choices, there are pros and cons to what we have covered here. A few of them are as follow:

PROs: When Applied

A. Those you surround yourself with will be trust-worthy;
B. You will choose those who have potential, are qualified, and are compatible;
C. Your mates will play their positions to the fullest;
D. Your business partners will pull their weight; and
E. Less chaos, even in your absence.

CONs: When Not Applied

A. Your other half will be your worst nightmare;
B. People on your team will fold under pressure, potentially causing your downfall;
C. Business partners will be lazy, incompetent, dis-content, and/or liabilities;
D. The tiger whose stripes you tried to change will stand true to its nature; and
E. Your carelessness will reflect upon and affect other relationships of yours negatively.

# 17 ESTABLISH YOUR ALLEGIANCES

*Allegiances will only last as long as the*
*interest of those aligned remains.*
—M.L. Walker Sr.

Let's be honest: most allegiances are fickle, to say the least. Most people will pledge allegiance to one thing today and then to the complete opposite tomorrow. The thing about this, however, is that allegiances are not a bad thing and are usually necessary when in pursuit of agendas. No matter if the cause is yours or someone else's, support is usually needed. So unlike the previous chapter, "Choose Your Partners Carefully," you really are not left with a choice of whether you need to align yourself or not, but rather to whom, what cause, and when.

Making these alliances is not something that should be taken lightly, and in all honesty should be approached in just as diligent a manner as discussed in "Choose Your Partners Carefully," if not more. The reasoning behind this is that causes are usually based on beliefs, and beliefs usually play vital roles in defining who we are as a person, most times extending down our family trees whether they support the same causes and share the same beliefs or not. Most times once you have allowed yourself to be attached to these causes or beliefs, it becomes nearly impossible to actually detach them from you.

In fact with today's society, this has become more true than it ever has been before, which means even after years or decades later, you may find yourself being forced to defend a cause you may no longer even support (if you ever did to begin with). Yes, imagine that. Just think of the countless politicians who, when attempting to take another stride on their life's journey, their past allegiances rise like a ghost of their past, lots of times actually becoming the death of very bright futures.

As haunting as the long-term effects can sometimes be, there are in fact allegiances that only last for short periods of time. The differences between short- and long-term allegiances are usually due to the agendas at hand, each party's importance to such, and the goals laid out when creating said alliances. I will now separate the two and go a bit more in depth.

## SHORT-TERM ALLIANCES

Sometimes a cause does not require a lengthy alliance as the resolution for the cause for which people align is something that can be easily achieved. In other cases the parties aligning themselves have different agendas tied to a common cause, which in turn means that once the person whose agenda is fulfilled first has seen said alliance through to this point, their vested interest is no longer the same as it was when entering into the alliance. Some may continue the course to its entirety if in fact they are truly dedicated to the actual cause at hand or have agreed to stay on through the other's course to completion. Yet this is usually unlikely due to the fact that most people who are in any real position to make worthy alliances more than likely have other phases to their agendas and therefore try not to be wasteful with their time, energy, or finances.

There are also instances where it is well understood when going in that certain parties are only as good as the purpose they serve, and although they would love to see the course through, to allow them to attempt doing so would not only be counterproductive but unwise. It should be noted that with the dissolving of these types of alliances (really any type, though the ending of long-term ones usually leaves unresolved issues), you should try to do so tastefully and on good terms, since you never know if further down the line, these other parties are once again needed to fulfill some repeat or new functions pertaining to your one-time alliance. One for sure method of doing this is never being afraid to give credit where credit is due. Well, that and the even better one of proper compensation when such applies, and yes, I too understand, with the greed of man, it is hard to reach the proper level, yet decent compensation beats zero compensation. The bottom line is that you just never want to leave too much room for error in regards to the work already put in, along with future plans that they may have been privy to in the process of fulfilling their functions. And yes, of course this applies to other partings as well, only we are dealing solely with alliances right now.

## LONG-TERM ALLIANCES

It is my belief that short-term alliances are more common than long-term ones, because long-term alliances usually have causes or agendas that are on a larger scale, more in depth and are time-consuming. So although they may require some individuals or groups to assist temporarily, those most likely to align themselves long term would be those most dedicated and/or suited to do so. When making these long-term allegiances, the parties involved are usually well aware of all the intricate details of what they are getting involved with, including the pros, cons, and what exactly will be expected of them each step of the way. Most times numerous meetings are held prior to, at the time of, and long after the agreements to align are finalized. This is especially the case when governments of countries decide to come together for a common cause or agenda.

Long-term alliances obviously can be some of the most complicated. The reason for this is the simple fact that as time goes on, things such as positions, conditions, and personal beliefs change. The problem is that those with whom these changes have taken place usually will be reserved about revealing anything of the sort (for just as many reasons as you would). Then there are, of course, some who will be quick to take a stance and voice their change of heart, but this is something that would usually be seen when the changes pertain to the cause or agenda which may now conflict with someone's personal position, condition, or belief. In addition, the harsh reality is that being loyal truly is not a common trait. So for individuals to remain true to a cause, agenda, or alliance for the long term is really a long shot (in the dark, I might add).

In fact the reality is that when truly aligning yourself with individuals or movements on a long-term situation, it would be best that your heart is in it one hundred percent, because usually that is exactly what will be at stake. See, this chapter would not be complete if I did not include the fact that some alliances, once the causes have been run, result in the extinguishing of any remaining parties aligned to parts others may never want attached to them ever again. You must enter every sincere alliance prepared to lay down your life as a party of it! Even if you are blessed enough not to became a loose end that needs tying, I would like to believe that you would be cautious enough not to spread yourself thin and only align yourself to individuals, causes, agendas, or movements for which you are sincerely prepared to give your very life! Since you should be aiming to win in all things you truly set your hearts to... what other way should you approach it, other than with everything inside of you?

# 18 PRIDE YOURSELF ON SEEKING KNOWLEDGE

*The more knowledge you obtain,
the better prepared you will be to
maneuver life's obstacles.*
—M.L. Walker Sr.

Though I have not been able to spend my entire life thus far engrossed in books or online sources seeking knowledge, I have always tried to keep my mind wide open, awaiting to soak up like a sponge any and all knowledge that became available for me to acquire. Odd as it is, my motivation was not due to the old cliché that knowledge is power. Do I believe that to be true? Absolutely. However, for me it was more to do with the semi-euphoric feeling I felt when I knew I had truly learned something interesting and worthy of being retained. The thing is that lots of what I would learn over the years would serve no other purpose for me than the quenching of my thirst for knowing more, which may very well be the case with lots more of what I learn in the days, weeks, months, and years to come. Nonetheless, I will have enjoyed filling my brain with things that bring me the pleasure of knowing. Ironically, even some of these things learned simply for the sake of acquiring knowledge can, and at times will, come in handy.

Lots of people spend their lives attempting to gain knowledge for no other reason than to try broadcasting all that they have learned to any and everyone they happen to come into contact with. These individuals tend to want to know all there is to know in the world and will eventually start to believe that they do. They will have answers for everything and will argue whoever disagrees into submission due to them not ever wanting to be incorrect, misinformed, or even slightly off-center. Well, I can tell you right now that this is not the purpose of this chapter and would strongly advise you, DO NOT become that person! Why? Because to become that person would only deprive you of so much more knowledge that, if only you were to humbly keep an open mind, would be readily accessible to you to soak up at will. Not to mention that eventually even when you are right and precise... no one will even care to accept what it is that you are offering as being valid and will quickly seek out another source to tap.

Knowledge to you should be invaluable, and for no other reason than there actually being no better way for us to spend this time that we have been fortunate enough to have, having been born into a world so beautiful and that offers so much for us to experience and learn from. I do not feel the need to explain things such as the birds soaring before the backdrop of fluffy white clouds in the baby-blue sky while the sun shines bright as ever... as surely they all speak for themselves. And if for some reason you have failed to stop and truly ponder thoughts on things of that nature, then you truly need to stop right now and try to take ten to twenty minutes just taking in these type of magnificent wonders. Then once you have done that, take just a few minutes to take note of all of the things men and women have created to mimic these marvels (at times down to the smallest details).

Now before I get any deeper off into this, there is something I must confess. Even though I am always open to seeking and accepting knowledge of any sort, I also make it my personal mission to let most of what I seek out be that which I feel can or will be of some type of assistance to me at some point. Basically when I am taking time out to apply myself, I pretty much look at that as an investment in myself. And since it usually entails extensive levels of digging, it would be safe to say that such time spent is more than likely taking away from something else that you could or would be doing. Plus, unless I have misunderstood the way things work, we usually invest with the hopes of such investments pushing out some form of a yield, and preferably with interest. The point I am trying to make is that it is okay to take time out to become knowledgeable on different subjects; however, when doing such starts to consume more time than you can afford to allow it to, then try to ensure that what you are spending that time gaining knowledge on is something with a strong possibility of allowing you to recoup on the time, energy, and (most likely) finances invested. I guess I just never understood those individuals who take trade after trade or course after course, for no other reason than obtaining a certificate or degree that they have little or no intentions of ever actually putting to use. In fairness, though, I'm sure most go in with the intentions of having purpose behind studying what they may.

Will we always be able to utilize the things that we become knowledgeable on? Realistically, no. Yet this should not discourage us from not only engaging in the process of continuous learning, but also encouraging those around us to do the same. Just the same, my not understanding why people acquire certificates or degrees they have no intentions of utilizing should not discourage anyone from achieving such goals. Why? Because even though these achievements may not be put to use formally or immediately does not mean that a person's time, energy, or funds were actually wasted, or that the knowledge gained will be useless. Sometimes the things we learn are meant to carry us throughout the course of our life, and most times it is the least expected time that the knowledge obtained, but thought useless, comes in handy. Most important is the fact that if we all just failed to continuously seek knowledge... then it would set in reverse all of the strides made as a civilization, as no one would be able to pass along the necessary information to continue to survive. This brings me to the next part of this chapter.

## PROMOTE EDUCATION

There has been and will continue to be campaigns to encourage education. These campaigns and movements have been geared towards each stage of the human life span and rightfully so, as not only is science and technology constantly improving, but the evolution of the world itself seems to be as consistent as its rotations, and appears that it will be that way until it ceases to spin. With this knowledge in mind, how could we not feel the duty to not only strive to learn and have readily available the knowledge to survive (not just in life but anywhere in this world), but also to promote the same to those around you, whom you should desire to survive and soar, as well.

Let us make no mistake about it... education is priceless! Unfortunately most governing bodies have chosen to undermine the ability of its people to equally engage in the learning process. Some will even go as far as minimizing the importance of not just education itself but the continuous furthering of such. Many will try to sell you on the idea of ignorance being bliss; however, anyone who attempts to do so actually does not have your best interest, and I am quite sure will show you differently in their actions regarding themselves and those whose best interest they do have at heart. Are there cases of individuals succeeding and prospering without utilizing the educational systems available? Absolutely. Yet even in those cases, I can assure you that more times than not, the very first chance those individuals got, they either began taking advantage of the educational outlets or surrounding themselves with people who had already done so. Why? Because the results of those who fail to do so is usually eminent.

I cannot tell you in what all ways you should promote education; however, I can say that if possible you should first lead by example, as no one ever really cares for others telling them what it is that they should or should not be doing, and especially so when that person fails to be a good representation of whatever it is that they are encouraging. It should also be noted that not everyone has the mental capability to take advantage of educational opportunities. Fortunately, though, in situations like that, there are ways for you to get around those issues, complaints, or arguments. First suggestion I would give would be to find out what the person you are interested in encouraging is interested in or would be suited for. Due to your observation and research for them, find out what would be required and maybe even some examples of others whom they can relate to. Secondly, if financially stable, investing in one's education is a sure shot way of not only showing them that education is as important as you say, but that you believe in them and their ability to make it work.

Just as some of the promoters of education will find themselves exempt from the learning process, we must keep in mind that some of those we would like to see become knowledgeable very well may fall into some of the categories that would either hinder them or make such impossible to the point of exemption. Yet and still, this does not remove our duty, and although we should always be considerate and never overbearing, there are always other means of being encouraging and supportive. Sometimes it may be something as simple as taking time out of our lives to teach individuals some of the basic things we have been fortunate enough to learn. Which highlights the fact that although most educational sources usually come with some form of financial obligations, there are usually affordable or even free alternatives. It is on us to be diligent in locating them when necessary.

## INFORMATION AND KNOWLEDGE IS POWER

So much in this world has been learned through trial and error, and even though this will be the case for a long time to come, the acquiring of all the information you can to build your knowledge up will give you the means to be effective, subsequently minimizing your errors and wastefulness. This is where real power comes into play, because when you are able to increase your effectiveness and minimize error and wastefulness... you ultimately increase your potential percentage for success in whatever it is that you are setting out to accomplish, and being able to repeat these results at will. Having such an advantage is powerful because time is money and errors are usually costly.

Yes indeed, information and knowledge can be utilized as power in too many other ways to count. Nonetheless, for this chapter I wanted to highlight information and knowledge being powerful in a non-manipulative manner. After all... blackmail, insider trading, and the selling of secrets are extremely dangerous criminal acts that I would not be able to encourage you to engage in, nor would I ever advise you to seek information or knowledge to gain that type of power. Why? Because it is not necessary. If you learn what you need to and apply it accordingly, then you will be the one who others would want to blackmail, or whose secrets they would hope to get to sell or trade. And if you have paid close attention to other chapters of this manual, then you will also be well prepared for those wishing to make you their victim, diminishing their success rate to the lowest percentage possible.

There was a reason why in ancient-time wars, one of the main agendas was to locate and destroy the libraries and other sources of knowledge while stealing, reworking, and taking credit for those items that would be most beneficial and/or progressive to them and their people. Just remember what type of power you choose to gain, how you choose to gain it, and what you choose to do with that power after you gain it is entirely up to you. As long as you continue to fulfill your duty to seek knowledge and then pass that knowledge along at some point... then it is my belief that you will have done your part to help those around you aid in the evolution of this beautiful world that we live in. I can only hope that it is for its growth and not its destruction.

# 19 THINK OUTSIDE OF THE BOX

*Many will try to keep your thoughts*
*contained. Don't you be one of them.*
—M.L. Walker Sr.

Sometimes governments, and at times even cultures and religions, thrive off of keeping multitudes of people boxed in mentally, and if that does not work, then physically, in hopes that a literally caged mind would then cease to grow and productively utilize itself. The thing is that we were given the ability to think, not to limit our range of our thought process but rather utilize it to the utmost of our ability, constantly testing the range to which we can push our mental capabilities to create, memorize, and resolve.

Unfortunately it takes all type of minds to make up a diverse world, so in taking this fact into account, as in the previous chapter, there are some that this will not apply to. For the rest of us, the only thing or person that can stop us from exercising our ability to think and not allow our minds to be boxed in is US! Most people are content with allowing others to think for them. In their minds they are allowing others to deal with the stress and suffer the headaches and lack of rest. But at what price? Then there are, of course, those who in fact do utilize their time and energy in thought, yet are afraid of the responsibility that comes with the revelation of what is behind the portals they happen to unlock. This therefore is for those of us who are capable and have the courage to not only unlock said portals of the mind but to travel to the distant plains and then challenge or allow it to go even deeper into the available layers in hopes of finding the answer to unanswered questions or resolution for any of our many issues of this world.

The following are some things that may prove helpful in allowing you to allow your mind to roam freely while harnessing your mental health and not allowing your thoughts to run away with you. Yes, I know you may feel as if I am being humorous, only I am not. Truth is that sometimes tapping into the genius inside of oneself will come at the price of their sanity. Most other times it will simply cause others to believe, make claims, and spread rumors of such, due to compulsive, neurotic, or aloof behavior patterns they will at times pick up through the course of their journey. And no, I personally am no genius, yet if I truly could tap into mine... then surely I would. For now, however, I will be thankful for simply being able and not afraid to think outside of the box.

## TAKE HEED TO WISDOM

Most people have the notion that they pretty much know it all, and since they know it all there is no reason to listen to or care about what the next person has to share. In fact some of you read this subtitle and immediately thought, "What does someone else's wisdom have to do with my thinking outside of the box?" Laughable, right? Well, to respond to what I suppose would be your random thought, I will say to you that history has a very funny way of repeating itself. And just as discussed in Chapters 14, "Learning From Your And Others' Mistakes" and 18, "Pride Yourself On Seeking Knowledge," the information, knowledge, and lessons of the past can prove extremely invaluable and beneficial for today and in the future.

Whenever you have the opportunity to receive something of substance from someone who is considered wise, you would be a fool not to take heed. Regardless of whether it immediately applies or not, it is good to always retain all that you can that may become useful at one point or another, because being able and willing to think outside of the box is only the beginning. The better informed you are, the greater the possibilities will be for the thoughts you come up with. The better informed your thoughts are, the greater chance you have of formulating something remarkable! And as much as I would like to tell you that just thinking outside of the norm is sufficient and acceptable... I would be lying to you. The truth is that ever since the discovery of fire and ways to control it, mankind's goal has been to continue striving in hopes of progressively evolving, subsequently raising the bar extremely high in this twenty-first century. It is for this very reason that all the help you can get will be needed, and the food for thought to ponder could prove fruitful and at times even priceless.

Does the bar being set so high and the need for your thinking outside of the box to have remarkable thoughts exclude you from exercising your ability and will to think outside the box? Absolutely not! Just as a seed buried in the earth must go through a process before it reveals itself and grows into what it will, most times the same applies to our thoughts. Therefore you should always apply yourself and exercise your ability and willpower to refuse to allow yourself to be mentally boxed in. Also, never forget that once it is known that this is your stance in life, there will be other forms of boxing you in that those who do not wish to see you excel will attempt to subject you to.

## DEFINE YOUR OWN RULES

Rules were created with no other purpose than to attempt to control people, processes, and courses of events. Some have been good while most have been self-serving with dire outcomes for those forced to follow them. I must agree that the whole concept of rules is in fact necessary; however, most times the powers that be cannot avoid abusing the structuring of the rules as well as to whom and how they are applied. And this is where the problems arise.

Now that we have covered a bit of the purpose and necessity of rules, I will explain what it is to define your own rules, and its relevance to this chapter. The first thing I need for you to understand is that even though thinking outside of the box is your personal prerogative, the effects of your doing so usually will reach others. Next you need to keep in mind that not all rules need changing, and for those that do, it would not be easy to do so. Therefore I suggest that in regards to this chapter, you do not focus on the changing of rules but rather the defining of your own. Does this mean you are to just go around making your own rules? No, not by far. What I am trying to convey to you is that once you begin to thinking outside of the box, you will then start to move throughout your life "outside of the box" in conjunction with your thoughts. This right here is why you will need to define your rules and why doing so is relevant to this chapter and manual.

Without defining rules for yourself to keep your thoughts, and actions that follow, as structured and precise as you can possibly get them, it will be impossible to acquire the levels of thinking outside the box that will be necessary, or to execute them effectively. If your desire is to control your thoughts and actions, maintain your mental stability, and reach your fullest potential, then it is a must you establish a set of guidelines for yourself to define the rules by which your thoughts and actions may one day be considered as representing. Simply put, find a way to contain your thoughts, the process, and how you constructively release them out into the universe. The end result is they will reflect upon you and your life's accomplishments.

# 20 LEARN HOW TO SACRIFICE

*Sacrifice is a humbling custom that most
find impossible to conform to. Embrace it
and become closer to your higher self.*
—M.L. Walker Sr.

The biggest problem with sacrifice is the fact that most people associate it with losing or forfeiting something unwittingly or by subtle force, though we all know that by all rights it is to relinquish on our own accord. I am guessing that by placing in one's psyche the unwillingness or quasi-forceful aspects, it allows justification for complaints, which in life will prove to be more common than not. Meaning (in short) that sacrificing is not something well liked by those who are to make the sacrifices, yet eagerly received by those who are to be the beneficiaries of the rewards from the sacrifice.

It takes a special type of person to become comfortable with sacrificing. The first thing that would be required is to gain a real understanding of the significance of sacrificing and how it will apply to you. It is my belief that in gaining an understanding of these things, you will come to view sacrifice as more of a tool that, when used wisely, will not only separate you from the pack character-wise, but will allow you to root out flawed characteristics of others.

Sacrificing is not something that should have to take place on a daily or regular basis, and therefore should not be confused with kind gestures or exchanges of assistance. The main things in regards to sacrificing are being able to first identify a sacrificial situation, knowing what position you take, to what extent, and finally... being able to actually follow through with the act when the time comes. This last part is the hardest for most people to overcome, since selfishness has become closer to the norm and an increase in fear of losing out or coming up on the short end of encounters and dealings has driven multitudes into shells.

The interesting thing about sacrifice is that its level of dimensions are unparalleled, which explains why we, so often, usually only hear it being spoken of in religious aspects (another reason why its correlation with elevation is high-lighted). Truth is pretty much anything can be sacrificed, from your feelings (i.e., your love, for someone else's happiness) to vested interests (i.e., equity, property, finances, etc., etc.).

There will be many who look down upon or attempt to discourage the act of sacrificing. Then there will be those who equate one's ability to sacrifice easily as those individuals being weak or easy to cave in. I personally think more thought and evaluating must be put into assessing individuals and situations prior to even beginning to pass that type of judgement, if in fact those individuals or situations hold that much of an importance in your life and whether or not you are even into passing judgement. But yes, weak people who easily cave in do exist; however, who is to say that they do not have their own reasoning for sacrificing in situations where that is actually the case?

In my opinion the world is a take, take, take, and little give place, or at least for the most part. So, with this being the case, it becomes necessary for some of us to acquire some type of "give" within our dealings with others. Acquiring the "give" does not mean that you would always be the one to accept the short end of sacrificial situations, but rather you will be the one to truly understand that sometimes it will take a person with the ability to sacrifice in order to allow things to move forward (hopefully achieving growth or progress in the process). Basically it becomes a tool that you use cautiously and as wisely as possible, because things that require sacrifice usually involve something of value to at least one of the parties involved, if not ALL. And therefore it is safe to say that sometimes there will arise occasions where it just honestly is not in one person or another's best interest to concede, and if that someone is you, then you had better know what could, should, and should not be sacrificed, when and how things of sacrificial nature should be entertained, and the pros and cons of whatever is at stake by even entertaining such. You must know your weaknesses and strengths, exactly what whatever is at stake means to you, and the probability of your being able to sway things in your favor (see Chapter 24 "Always Be About Your Business," under the subtitles "Learn The Art Of Negotiating" and "Learn The Art Of Persuasion"). The fact is that sometimes it is simply best to allow someone else to mediate or do your bidding for you. No matter the case, being honest with yourself is most important and a must!

One of my favorites about sacrificing is "Sacrificing To Succeed." This is basically when I sacrifice something big or small for something that appears (and may actually be) small, less valuable, or useless to the other party, yet is a very intricate piece to a puzzle or two. Letting go is not something I believe is easy for anyone and therefore I have not been exempt, yet once 1 commit mentally, I try to relent without dwelling on what I have sacrificed. The main thing about sacrificing is that there is no taking them back once they have been made, so what would be the point in continuing to dwell on them? I usually like to get right to putting the pieces in place to complete whatever puzzle the sacrifice was designed to complete. Of course my visions will not always materialize into the works of art I would like, only since I am more content with a fail as opposed to a failure to attempt... I have learned to live with whatever the end results are.

# 21 BUILD YOUR TEAM EFFECTIVELY

*To reach one's true potential usually*
*requires assistance, and those assembled*
*will only be as effective as he or she*
*who brings them together.*
—M.L. Walker Sr.

There is a good reason why ninety-nine percent of the time when someone is being celebrated, that person tries to ensure that the proper credits are given to those around them who helped make it all possible. Yes, it is good to have the heart, willpower, talent, or character of ten individuals; however, when attempting to accomplish something worthy of being notable, it will usually require a team of individuals because the harsh reality is that individually we all still equal only one person and have been designed to only do so much. Even the rarest of us will only be able to accomplish so much and more than likely will end up needing someone else (who themselves may also end up needing assistance) in order to make what you are focused on happen. Especially if you want positive results.

The teams you put together or become a part of will be a representation of you, as you will them. Sometimes teams will shift, splinter, or be numerous, with each serving different purposes or having different goals. Some of the related issues to keep in mind pertaining to this were already covered in a number of previous chapters and will be further discussed in a couple of the remaining chapters, because although this manual deals mainly with you being or becoming the best, or better, you... most of us will be nothing without the teams we build around us and depend upon to see our visions or blueprints into fruition.

Most ethnic groups' and/or culture's success can be attributed to them picking their teammates from within their ethnic group, culture, or family. Unfortunately, that is not always the winning recipe for everyone, and therefore we are left to find other ponds from which to pull the pieces that will best suit our needs. It is for these reasons that those of you who assume the responsibility of building and/or nurturing teams must truly understand the little things that most would usually overlook when bringing people together. Truth is, you would be amazed at how many people assume that simply finding a body to fill the space of a necessary function is all it takes. I personally have been guilty of such myself. Yet once you get over that part, along with the concern of hurting someone's feelings, due to your needing to pick and place accordingly, then you will be on your way to doing great things!

Now as you should already know from Chapter 16 "Choose Your Partners Carefully," picking those to team up with is crucial and should be done with the utmost care. However, there are still some very important things that must be heeded and approached with just as much care. Unfortunately these situations usually tend to involve some trial and error, as rarely will any of us put together or become a part of a perfect team right out the gate. With this being said, there will usually be a lot of alternating, rethinking, and replacing, and this may very well be the case for the duration of the team's existence. Still in all, it is our duty to cover all the bases reasonably possible in attempt to increase the percentage of successfully bringing together a group of individuals who will be highly compatible and effective in accomplishing the things that you all come together with goals to achieve. And it is with these facts in mind that I go into the other things of importance you will need to factor into your team-building process.

## TEACH YOUR TEAM

A team member who has not been properly taught truly cannot be at fault when their functions are not properly performed. So easily we assume that just because a person has a title or position, they automatically know everything that such title or position entails and will be able to fulfill their responsibilities to the necessary standards. Yes, I agree that for the most part, everyone should try to always know what is required of them in these situations, yet knowing what is required and knowing how to fulfill that requirement is still two different things, and the only way to prevent this from becoming an issue is to teach your team what it is they need to know or ensure that they are being properly taught and/or trained in the necessary fields for which they will be responsible.

Teaching even a child can be either a tedious or easygoing process, so surely nothing different can be expected with youth, young adults, or adults. No matter the case, your approach should be a humble one, as being patient and under-standing usually allows the student to be more comfortable and open to the whole process. In addition to being receptive in regards to what they are being taught, it is very possible they would be more honest with themselves and you as to their true capabilities, which is usually not an easy thing to do with people who truly want to be useful and a part of a team. Plus it is important to keep in mind that although being a part of a team is serious business (be it sports, business, or whatever you may), you should always try making it a supportive and positive experience, which should start with the learning aspect.

Something else to consider here is actually having a core function manual that could cover all of the basics in every field that play a vital role in whatever your team has been formed to partake in, and ensuring that everyone is at least schooled on the basics covered within so that for any circumstances requiring a substitute, there will be someone already on the team available and prepared to fill in. Of course there will always be some functions that cannot be substituted, and for those situations you would at least try to have an emergency alternative or back-up plan for everyone to be taught how to implement, if ever a time arises wherein such becomes necessary. And if any of your team is not eager to learn all there is to know about whatever it is you all have formed together for, then are they even a good fit or worthy of a position?

## TEST YOUR TEAM

As you may very well know, or will soon find out, people will tell you anything, commit to anything, and swear to their abilities, simply to be a part of something, and ten times faster if there is some type of incentives involved. In addition to that, we could spend a lifetime teaching and trying to prepare individuals to perform well in their fields or positions, but all could very well be for naught if we are not testing those individuals to ensure that not only is the knowledge being retained, but that their skills are up to par to properly fulfill their responsibilities as a team player.

It is my belief that it should not be made a secret that testing of one's knowledge and abilities will take place at some point. This does not mean that you should not slip in some unannounced or unexpected test later on in time to evaluate their reactions, performance, and efficiency. Giving notice that the possibility of such type of test regarding their knowledge and skills to ensure the strength and efficiency of you all as a team should leave no one with any reason to feel blindsided, ambushed, or unfairly treated. It should not be necessary for nonstop random testing, since either they will get it or not, you will trust in their abilities or not, or you will build resentment and discourage them. However, do not hesitate to continuously teach and test them (annually, bi-annually, or as needed) in order to stay current on things to keep you all competitive and up to par standard-wise.

As with the teaching, your approach should be a humble one, yet firm in the testing designed and executed. Quite naturally you cannot have easy designs or turn blind eyes towards the executing phases if you intend to attain notable achievements. Still in all, you can get the desired results by being understanding, humble, and ensuring that your position is solely about the betterment of the team and its objective. And although there will always be some disgruntled potential teammates who fail to make the cut, your manner of teaching, testing, and relieving those who do not qualify will sometimes make all the difference.

## DEMAND PROPER REPRESENTATION

Getting people to represent you or your team as you do, or envision it should be done, will be an extremely complicated task, though not an impossible one. The biggest hang-up here will be individuality, as we have been programmed to take pride in individualism, and when attempting to bring numerous individualistic characteristics in concert, the diversity of those involved may conflict. For those of you who encounter a situation whereas everyone instantly meshes, be thankful as that will be the equivalent of hitting a mega-millions lottery. For the rest of you, be prepared to work hard, constantly, and diligently, as I have had to, in hopes of finding those who truly understand the importance of representing one another, and the team as a whole, properly.

Amazingly you will have those who purposely do things to misrepresent you and/or your team, when they get it in their head that you do not see them as a good fit or are already aware that they lack the morals, character, or endurance and know the end result of such coming to the light and being recognized. The best remedy for situations of this nature is to separate yourself and/or the team from whoever it is who decides misrepresentation is acceptable, and remain unyielding in demanding that proper representation is displayed by yourself (as surely you must lead by example) and those who are truly dedicated to being a team player and representing such accordingly.

## LET THOSE AROUND YOU PROSPER

One of the leading causes of dysfunction, outside of failing to adhere to the subjects above, is refusing to allow those on your team and closest to you to make progress and prosper. This is something that keen attention will be given to, not only by your teammates but those closest to you all as well. Do not misread what I am getting at here because everyone should still have to earn their keep, as opposed to wanting or receiving handouts. What I am, however, trying to enlighten you to is the fact that being supportive of the growth of your teammates can only be beneficial to them, you, and the team as a whole. Just as your placing ceilings on or hindering their growth only does the same to yourself and the team alike.

Will everyone grow and prosper equally? Not likely. Yet and still, your mission ought to be ensuring that the opportunity is presented for each of those with a position on your team to develop, grow, and prosper, as well as to encourage them to take advantage of those opportunities. Now of course, from that point on, it will be entirely up to those individuals what they decide to do and what amount of growth and prospering suits them, but no matter their decision or the end results... you will have done your part.

## APPLY RULES EQUALLY

Favoritism can be detrimental to the meshing, growth, progress, and success of a team, and this is especially so when it applies to the implementation and enforcement of rules. For ages those in power, authority, or control have implemented laws and rules that are biased, self-serving, and disparaging. And although it propelled many to wealth and power, the resentment, dislike, and hatred it fostered at times proved to be more trouble than one had bargained for, with more final results yet to be seen. Of course you will not be able to appease everyone involved, yet as long as you create and apply rules fairly, then it will be hard for anyone to have valid complaints. You may even consider allowing everything to be a combined effort, so decisions are made as a whole and no fingers can be pointed or accusations of inequality levelled.

You never want the people you will depend on to make wheels turn to feel as if they are being treated unfairly or having rules enforced against them unequally. To do so would only create situations that will eventually cause a breakdown within the team, which will subsequently have a negative effect on the team's ability to be productive and successful at accomplishing the goals you all set out to accomplish. See, even if a person does not like being reprimanded, if they know that it is for the betterment of the team, and the rules being enforced are not being applied unequally... they will more than likely attempt to be understanding and respect such. Once again, all you can do is to do your part to make sure equal treatment is being given, and from there simply be prepared to deal with matters however necessary.

# 22 PLAY YOUR HAND ACCORDINGLY

*Most times you will only get one chance to*
*play your hand out, best make it count.*
—M.L. Walker Sr.

The majority of us get one life to live, and even for those who are fortunate enough to get a second chance or continuance of one cut short, the goal is usually the same... live it as best they can, for themselves and (usually) those held close to heart. A common expression for this is "playing the hand you were dealt," which is associated with "playing cards" and the many games that are played with them (usually poker). The outcome of which is a person or team either wins, loses, or draws (i.e., tie, leaving a contest undecided), and where, whether individually or as a team, the hand you are dealt and the way you decide to play it is indispensable.

To stay on course with the analogy given, some of the players in this game of life will resort to becoming tricksters or swindlers, with gimmicks, schemes, and stratagems of deception, with hopes of either sleight-of-handing or bluffing their way to the top (winning). While others will take the time to educate themselves, honing their crafts along the way until they are confident in their ability to play the game, maneuvering the circuits, fully aware of when to hold them, fold them, to walk away or run (of which Kenny Rogers's classic speaks). And since it can be said that success has been obtained through either of these paths (depending on what one considers success), it will be on you to figure out which route is best suited for you.

With that made clear, we will begin to cover some of the pivotal points that will play vital roles in your playing your hand in life accordingly. There is no set order that these go in, but it is my position that all should be read and given the proper consideration.

## USE GIFTS YOU WERE BORN WITH

We all were born with some type of gift or another. Sometimes it will be as obvious as could be and at other times it will take time to develop and reveal itself. With this being the case, it would only be natural for you to at least be able to identify your gift or potential gifts, so that you can better understand not only the gifts but yourselves as well. By gaining an in-depth understanding of your gifts, you will hopefully begin to realize your true potential.

Even after you have realized and begun to gain an understanding of said gifts, it will still take time and effort, for those of us who are not naturals, to learn how to utilize these gifts in our lives to help advance us forward. In fact it is pretty much the same as we have witnessed in comic books, or the movies adapted from such, where the superheroes or villains come into realization that they have a gift or power. It's very rare that any of them are immediately aware of what exactly the gift is or how exactly to use it. In fact very few even know how to harness them initially, and it is this task that they are first saddled with. It is also around this stage when one is to decide whether it will be the good or bad that they choose to use their gift or power for, just as you will have to decide what yours will be used for. And clearly you should be made aware that even though your gifts may help put you in positions of power... they will not be superpowers as in the comics or movies. So please do not take that mental trip, but rather stay grounded and focused, and make the gifts you possess work for you.

## CALCULATE ALL OF YOUR MOVES

The worst thing you could ever do is be an impulsive person. Not only does an impulsive person fail to put much (or any) thought into their actions or reactions, they are usually driven by their emotions and take unnecessary risks. These are recipes for disaster and as opposed to increasing their odds in favor of success, they increase them for failure.

I once read something very interesting about the "One Percent" of people in the world who retain the labels of being the most wealthy people in the world today and subsequently controlling everything around us. What I read was that most of them take chances just as you and I, but the only difference between us and them is the fact that the chances they take are calculated chances. This made so much sense, because growing up we would mostly make moves just to keep things in motion, and even when I did begin putting more thought into my movements, I did not calculate as deeply as I should have. Truth is I was content with the results I was receiving and, like most who have dwelled in the urban trenches, could not begin to think to far ahead. Luckily this is not the case with you all and therefore you all should always be looking five and ten years down the line, lining your movements up to be consistent with such.

Does putting thought into calculating your movements guarantee you will be successful in whatever endeavors said movements pertain to? Not hardly. However, I can say in all honesty that it should without question increase the likelihood of you edging the odds in your favor. And then it will be on you to actually capitalize on the edge that you have managed to gain.

## WEAR YOUR MASK WELL

Although I have never been a big fan of wearing masks myself, I am very aware of the necessity to be able to pull off the wearing of such, when times call for it. There can be many reasons that call for these metaphorical masks to be picked up, only I would suggest that you never make it such a habit that you lose your true identity due to constant donning of masks. Nevertheless, when the time does come for you to wear one, be sure to become one with it.

## TRUST IN YOURSELF WHEN OTHERS DO NOT

It is very hard to get others to believe and trust in you and your abilities. In fact most people would rather bet against you, even if they are aware of your dedication and/or will-power. The thing about this is that even though it would be nice to have others believe and trust in you (especially those closest to you)... you should never become dependent on such to the extent to where it becomes the determining factor as to whether or not you prevail. The bottom line is that YOU have to be willing to trust and believe in yourself wholeheartedly! Even if at the time you find yourself being the only one who does.

## USE WHAT OTHERS USE AGAINST YOU TO YOUR ADVANTAGE

Throughout life there will be too many people to count who will attempt to gather information or knowledge on you, your strengths, and your weaknesses, with no other intention than to one day be able to use this information or knowledge against you. Some will be so diligent that they will go to the end of the world if need be to accomplish their goal. And no... they will not always appear in wolves' clothing, but rather will usually appear as sheep or doves, until it is time for them to strike (or you get wise to their true character).

Now that we know people will try to come for us in many disguises with ill intent, the million-dollar question is how to use that to our advantage. To answer this I will first have to say that there is no one set way, and the truth is that you will have to learn how to master a number of things covered in this manual, and especially those highlighted in this chapter. I like to think back to the epic rap battle in the movie *8 Mile* when the white rapper B-Rabbit knew how his opponent would attempt to tear him down for being white and poor, but had gained the information of the opponent's perpetrating the fraud of coming from a life of hardship in the ghetto when in fact, despite his convincing appearance of such, he had come from the easy side of the tracks. Back to reality with it: if you identify and learn to use the gifts you were born with, calculate your moves, wear your mask well, and trust in yourself when engaging... then at the very least you will be able to rest knowing that you played your hand as accordingly as you possibly could have.

DO NOT HALF-STEP

Something else you need to be enlightened on is the fact that in this game of life, *YOU* CANNOT HALF-STEP! Under no circumstances are you to take this marvelous experience that you have been so fortunate to have been granted lightly. You have this one life to live and you should have every desire to make the very most of it you possibly can! Yes, you should enjoy it just as much along the way, only play your hand accordingly so your options will be limitless. The way I see it, going only halfway is next to nothing. And yes, sometimes life itself will intervene, only that is simply how life works. This is exactly why you are being provided with this manual, because with this and your endurance built up... you have nothing but WINNER written all over your face.

# 23 MASTER THE ART OF INTERACTING

*If communication is the key, then
interacting is the Master Key. Master it
and enter a new realm of life.*
—M.L. Walker Sr.

This is an area in which I confess even I myself have a very long way to go to just begin finessing, let alone mastering. My weakness in this area is not due to unawareness of what it takes to interact, but rather my inability to easily interact with those I truly care less to interact with. As noted in the previous chapter (subtitle "Wear Your Mask Well"), I never cared for wearing masks and therefore since most of these situations would actually require me to do so, I usually opt out and find alternative routes to whatever the purpose of the interactions are. I stand on my position because it is who I am as a person, insofar as being one who is willing to live with some of my faults, as opposed to seeking perfection within my pursuit of self-betterment. Yet and still, I am well aware that for those who have the ability to properly balance interacting with whomever, whenever, and wherever, while staying true to themselves and not compromising their morals, integrity, or character... there shall be very few doors that will not open wide for them.

## LEARN WHO PEOPLE ARE

We have covered many subjects that pertain to this subtitle throughout this manual. I reiterate it here and now because it is imperative that you understand just how much people truly do not like for others to be able to see and know them for exactly who they are. What is very odd about this is the fact that this does not mean the person is a bad individual or that their desire to keep particulars of themselves under wraps is due to anything negative about them.

The fact is that the majority of people understand that privacy is the first and last line of security. The less a person knows about you and your private life, the harder it becomes for that person to violate you. Ironically this even applies to some of our closest relationships, whereas we only want for people to see as much as we see fit. This does not imply that there is anything insincere about these relationships, but simply a sign of the lengths that we will go to protect ourselves (emotionally, mentally, and physically). See, the more we open ourselves up, the more vulnerable and susceptible we are to different things that others may decide to interject into our lives. And I know the first thought that comes to mind is the fact that those closest to you should never want to bring anything harmful into your life, yet the problem here is that people change and even those closest to you are not exempt. In addition to people changing, the harsh reality is that others just do not always have our best interest at heart, no matter if we have theirs or not.

Now that we know why it is that people do not care to allow others to learn who they are and that they will go to many different lengths to maintain control over what they allow to be revealed, we now have a clearer understanding of the work that will need to be put into peeling back layers on top of layers of these individuals' identity. There are a number of methods that must be considered, as covered in Chapters 5, 7, 11, 13, 15, 18, 19, and 22.

## TRY NOT TO BE DESPISED

I cannot say that being the friendliest person on the earth is the way to go, only can say with absolute certainty that you never want to be despised. Be displeasing, disfavored, or even disliked, but never despised. A person who has the ability to allow themselves to become despised is a person who will always have an issue with interacting with others. Why? Because to accomplish this usually requires for a person to have compromised their character by being in moral turpitude, at which point the aura that person starts to give off in their encounters is one of negative vibrations. Yes, of course there will be some who are able to pull off being able to interact well although they are morally bankrupt; however, they are usually people who have already been accustomed to interacting, and upon deciding to use their abilities for immoral purposes, found ways to mask the negative vibes. Yet and still, even those skilled at masking the aura will slip up and find themselves being loathed and despised.

Does being despised mean that a person will not accomplish goals or even become successful? I would have to say no. Also, although most of these type of successes are usually short-lived, there are some who defy the odds and have had extensive runs. Not that such have not come at what would be considered a grievous price to those of us who still have some good inside of us, only for those who have abandoned all good left of them, things of such consequential effects are not of a concern.

I am figuring that you yourself can think of numerous reasons why you or anyone else should not want to live a life as a person who is despised. However, I am going to still express to you my reasoning. In addition to all the many reasons that you all could so easily run off, to be a person who is despised would make it next to impossible to be successful at not only digesting much of the life lessons embodied in this writing, but at executing some of the most important elements. Personally I do not think that a despised person truly cares much about being or becoming a better person, and therefore would not be very motivated to apply himself or herself, which in turn will usually result in a walking definition of Murphy's law (what can go wrong will), as "no one" will want to be a part of the energy that comes along with that, resulting in loss of opportunity.

# 24 ALWAYS BE ABOUT YOUR BUSINESS

*If business truly is a combination of war and*
*sport, and a battle of wits... why then*
*wouldn't you approach it as naturally as*
*you intake the air you breathe?*
—M.L. Walker Sr.

In this chapter we will go over a number of subjects that are all interrelated and, no matter what your business is, it would be wise of you to take heed to this chapter and all that it covers, as anything less than being about your business will almost certainly result in less than remarkable outcomes. Some of you may think that you will be just fine with mediocre results out of life, since surely everyone cannot live remarkable lives, only once you have had a chance to live and witness the look of defeat in the eyes of another, I can almost assure you that from that day forward, you will strive to be the best you that you ever could be! And it is at this time that you will come to the realization that there is truly only one way for that to be possible... hence the title of this chapter.

As with most of the things in this manual, a lot of what follows will not be easy and will require a lot of self-discipline and willpower. Interestingly, you will find that nearly all of the days of your life will be spent attempting to master this art, as it is within it that our progress, prosperity, and rewards will usually be revealed. With that being said, we should find resolve in opening our minds to accepting the fact that most things we ever want to accomplish will usually only come into fruition throughout the course of us being about our business.

## STUDY YOUR CRAFT

Knowing what it is you are good at is always a good thing. Sometimes these things will be natural talents, and other times interesting hobbies that turn serious. Either way, once our talents are realized or honed in on, it then becomes our duty to fully understand as much as we possibly can about such and the ways that we can become well rounded in exercising them.

Studying your craft is really no different than studying for a test or anything else that requires proper preparation in order to achieve a positive outcome. The only difference is that in this case what you are studying to achieve is something that should not only be useful for a long time to come, but should also help you accomplish all that you seek to accomplish.

No one should ever have to force you to treat your craft seriously, since if you yourself are serious about being respected in whatever your field happens to be, then that in itself would be enough to cause you to approach it in a studious fashion. The objective is to become so skillful at your craft that it feels as if you could actually do it with ease in your sleep. And then you double back around for a deeper level of understanding and training of it and/or those areas directly related, utilizing whatever time or means necessary to help you get to this stage, which will separate you from everyone else in your field.

## KEEP FAMILY AND BUSINESS SEPARATE

This is a very sensitive subject since not only does family sometimes play a crucial role in the initial stages of whatever our business may be, they also seem to take on a sense of entitlement due to family ties alone. Most would agree that dealing with family is hard enough without adding the elements of business, yet there are those who are in a form of business whereas the only people they could honestly trust are their family members. So in figuring out where you stand in regards to this subject, you must first be clear with yourself as to which of these models you are working off of and who all can be trusted most to aid you in accomplishing the goals to bring forth success.

I have dealt with this issue for quite some time now and am just now getting to the point of being able to distinguish who is best suited to be of assistance to me and my causes. My hangup over time has been not ever truly trusting anyone outside of my family, and therefore figured that some form of family needed to be included no matter what I was working on. I could not have been more wrong, as not-so-good fits are just not-so-good fits, no matter how much we try to force them to be otherwise.

One of the simplest things to do to resolve this issue is to never go against your initial instinct. If your inner self is second-guessing your even having the idea, then that is usually a telltale sign that it's a bad idea. And just in fairness, if you decide to go against your better judgement for the sake of not being judgmental (which, by the way, you have every right to do when it's your time, energy, and finances being invested), then start out with small, non-essential functions to see how seriously they take said assignment and level of responsibility. If in fact that goes well, then you can begin to allow them to work their way up, because in all honesty to create a circle of constructive economics would absolutely be nice, and is a desire we all tend to usually share in common. However, it is our relatives who must understand their roles in these designs to create wealth, build stability, or grow in power.

## DO NOT GET INVOLVED IN THINGS YOU CANNOT CONTROL

What I am attempting to break down to you is not about being a control freak or whatever one may call it, but rather an attempt to get you to exercise more control over the things that you involve yourself with. Exercising more control over what you involve yourself in would usually empower you to have some type of control (if not total) of how they turn out. No, there is no guarantee that this will be the case; however, when you use common sense and have the ability to refrain from giving in to peer pressure, this should increase the probability that you will be able to dictate and stand firm regarding the positions you take or things you are or are not comfortable with being in or a part of. That in itself will play a major role in the things in which you involve yourself.

There will always come times where you just happen to find yourself involved in things that you will have little to no control over. In these instances the wisest thing to do would be to remain in control of your demeanor and actions, and analyze the situation in hopes of finding an angle from which you may possibly be able to actually gain control, or at least some type of control.

There are numerous chapters here that touch on your being aware and tapping into your innermost being, and all of these things play a crucial part in what all you allow yourself to get involved with. The other part is simply being able to think for yourself and having a voice to say no. You have to know what you are and are not willing to get involved in, and if you exercise zero control of what you allow yourself to get involved in, then surely you have a long road ahead of you, or maybe I should say a rather short one.

## LEARN THE ART OF NEGOTIATING

When it comes to making deals, most people will live or die by the code of starting big and reluctantly lowering when selling, and inching upward after starting low when buying. Of course these are bonafide methods of negotiating that have been proven time and again throughout the ages. Truth is, however, that to be a true negotiator takes a lot more than just exercising the high/low technique, and this is why it is described as an art in the subtitle.

For starters I would like for you to think about the words *barter*, *haggle*, and *compromise*. If need be, take a little time to gain an understanding of the fundamentals of each one. When thinking of them, I want you to first do so individually and then combined. Find the correlation of the three and how they could be of assistance to you in relation to this art.

The reason I have focused so much on these three words is because to become a true artist of negotiating would require you to first familiarize yourself with the juggling of said acts. Next your task would be to gain an understanding of when it is time for each to be exercised, and finally for you to do so as efficiently and tactfully as possible.

It is my belief that being a good negotiator is knowing what to give, how much to give, when to give, and how to give it... all while ensuring with absolute certainty that you receive all that you seek and more or, at the very least, close enough to such that you are comfortable with the results. And here is the most interesting part: you are to do all of that while managing to complete the negotiations with all parties involved being content with the outcome at the end. But please know that just because everyone is content at the completion of negotiations does not mean that they will remain that way, so try to be sure that in the process of completing the different phases of negotiating, you cover the necessary bases to keep you from being the party who is later dissatisfied. (See also Chapter 20 "Learn How To Sacrifice.")

## LEARN THE ART OF PERSUASION

Being able to persuade someone to bend towards your will or point of view is a very powerful ability. Clearly this goes hand in glove with negotiating; however, being that it can be applied to so much more, I felt it necessary to avoid allowing its depth to get lost within being a supporting role of another art. I mean to be able to sway another person's thoughts, opinions, and/or beliefs is very dangerous, for two reasons. The first is that once you are able to sway a person's thoughts, opinions, and/or beliefs, you will subsequently have had some effect on how it is they think or live their life, and very possibly some of the things they will do throughout their lives.

And without fail, the second reason gets even more interesting because it does not involve the person you have persuaded, but rather you yourself being the person doing the persuading. Wielding the ability to influence people's lives and actions is one of the rawest forms of power, and as with any source of power, be it energy or strength, if not handled with safety and caution, it can be extremely harmful and deadly! And therefore it is imperative that the more skillful you become at exercising this art, you do so with caution, care, and consideration, because unlike negotiations that usually conclude upon the completion of the task, persuasion will, more times than less, have longer effects and the potential to spread.

Clearly one would assume there are many different levels of persuasion; however, I give you the core essence of the art, its capabilities and effects, because the smallest uses of it can and will snowball into something bigger. Whether it be good or bad, and to what extent it will grow is usually unknown (no matter our desire), and it is for this reason we should never take or exercise the art of persuasion lightly. Power unharnessed is explosive, and it is without question that influence equates power. Which is why I will bring this subject to a conclusion without giving right and precise techniques to aid you.

My position is this: I have given you more than enough insight in this manual to assist you with learning and becoming skillful in persuasion. Either you are gifted or able to become skillful at applying the art, or you are not. Surely this ability is not meant for everyone, and since it will be a task for even the gifted or skillful to adequately harness such, it would be absolutely ludicrous to think those who were never meant to wield such power would utilize it accordingly.

## IN GOOD TIMES, PREPARE FOR THE BAD

So often we procrastinate and put things off for later dates in anticipation of what will supposedly take place tomorrow, and this is especially so when things are going good and looking up. This has been very detrimental to not only myself but many others, as very few are taught early on about properly preparing for bad times. We take for granted the fact that things could never always remain good and therefore the bad times have no choice but to rear their ugly heads.

For starters let's get something understood. You have to first have something (or figure out a way to get something so that you will have something) to be able to begin preparing with. Whatever it is you are to acquire is unspecified, because almost anything could be of value, and so although the primary goal would be financial earnings, it will take something to bring the finances to you. Maybe it's a job, gift, or even an idea. No matter the case, adding on to it will not be easy, because the more of it you get, the more things you or the people around you will come up with for you to do with it, and rarely will that be to save it.

Now whether your "something" is money, property, intellectual property, natural or unnatural resources, you should make it a habit early on of setting something to the side in preparation for hard times. Maybe it will be a savings account, 401k, stocks and bonds, precious stones, or metals; however, you must find a means of saving a portion of it or the proceeds from it for a rainy day. In addition to your making this a habit, it is a lesson that you will want to pass down to your children, children's children, and loved ones in general, beginning with the piggy banks, savings accounts, and more tangible things that will preserve or increase in value, plus always be of use to someone.

It should also be noted that there are other ways of preparing for hard times. Most of us look at people who prepare for natural disasters or catastrophic events (survivalists and preppers) as being foolish or looney; nevertheless, with all of the natural and unnatural disasters that have been transpiring more often around the world, I think it is safe to say that maybe they are actually onto something. Ironically, pickling, drying, and stockpiling food and essentials not too long ago was the norm, and in fact has been making a comeback along with gardening. Luckily we now have even more advanced things to aid us in being prepared, only I would not stop at just canned goods, bottled water, candles, batteries, and generators. Truth is there is a lot to learn from watching or reading up on survivalists and preppers. Not to mention that even bunkers for the masses have become more affordable.

## LEARN HOW AND WHEN TO INVEST

There is a saying, "Never chase bad money with the good," and boy, do I wish someone had opened my eyes wide to it long before I poured so much of it down the drain. But hey, it is what it is, and sometimes when you get caught up in the enjoyment of having your own money to do whatever it is that you desire, you may think about tomorrow but very rarely the following week, month, year, or decade. Yes, I understood that it took money to make more money, and that I should allow the money to work for me; nonetheless, I failed to properly apply these things correctly or in the correct fields, otherwise I would have had a different approach to what I invested in, how and when... which by this time would have allowed me to master the art of moving money worldwide.

It used to be a time where a person's choices of investing revolved around food, housing, clothing, transportation, and energy. Today that is no longer the case, as there are way too many options available to even begin to count. And just as always, not all of the available options are good ones, which means you will first need to figure out which ones are most logical and which you would be most comfortable with.

Once you have figured out the things you would feel most comfortable investing in, you will want to do some research on it to get some type of understanding of its past, present, and potential future in hopes of making the proper predictions of when and what to invest. In all honesty, knowing the things I do, I would say to research it thoroughly as well as some closely related items or areas, as this would possibly give you more insight on its sustainability and growth potential. It should also enlighten you as to whether your investment should be long or short term.

Learning how exactly you should invest into things is very important and is something you should spend time studying. There are many different ways to approach investing; however, you should never go outside of what you are comfortable with. I cannot tell you how you should go about it because sometimes it will make sense to invest big while other times it would be wisest to invest small or pass altogether. The fundamentals are essential and once you have a good understanding of them, there will be only one other thing to get a handle on.

Timing is usually everything when it comes to investing. When you should proceed and when you should pull out are key factors of whether or not you will earn profits or lose your investment. Naturally whatever it is you are investing in will play a major role in when you should invest as well, being that some things are seasonal or may have a short shelf life. Then you have some things that are simply best caught at the ground level prior to peaking or spiraling. With this in mind, be precise in your timing of executing your investing or cashing out of investments.

## DO NOT WASTE YOUR RESOURCES

The harsh reality is that resources just do not come easily or constantly, and since they do not come in that fashion, why would we easily expend them? Or let me put it this way: Not only are resources hard to come by, they are usually limited. Now I once again put said question before you... why then would we easily expend them? Exactly, we should not!

Resources come in many different forms, ranging from personal skills or connections, to your food, gasoline, and all else that falls in between this category. People will always attempt to tap you for your resources and, amazingly, if you would be foolish enough to continue to part ways with or expend your resources, they will tap you for them until there is nothing left. Your resourcefulness could become a source of wealth or empowerment itself, yet whether it does or does not, there will be many around you, as well as afar, who will seek to run you dry of your resources. And I can assure you with complete certainty they will be less inclined to make available or extend to you theirs. Sound familiar? Want access to yours but will not give access to theirs, will borrow yours but not want to lend theirs.

Resources are to be used and shared wisely. To do otherwise is a direct attack on your and your rightful dependents' well-being, stability, and growth. So preserve your resources, use them mainly when necessary, and allow only the worthy access to them, and surely you will see positive results. And do not fret over being liked or disliked, because most people will smile in your face and utilize your resources, while never truly caring for you to begin with. All the yes-men and boot-lickers will still kiss up to you, as your resources will increase instead of decreasing, and they will all hold on to the hopes of their potential favor. So your ego will continue to be appeased (if you happen to be shallow enough to need such); just allow it to do so while preserving your resources and resourcefulness. Make people bring something to the table as tokens of good faith, even if it's simply resources of their own.

## BUSINESS AND CONFLICT DO NOT MIX

Unless you happen to be in the business of war, conflict is nothing more than unnecessary distractions. Yes, business is very hectic and warlike; however, being competitive and aggressive in your business model or practices is different than engaging in or entertaining actual conflict. Being distracted by conflict can be costly, and the losses you will suffer will almost be for certain if you allow conflict to make its way into your business.

No matter what your business is, your duty is to keep it on course. Under no circumstances are you to allow nonsense to derail you or stop your momentum and/or growth. You will find that too easily others will attempt to interject nonsense into your business affairs, yet this is simply to cause conflict and you should not fall victim to it. If and when the time comes whereas remaining focused and staying the course is made impossible and conflict seems unavoidable... then deal with it accordingly and show your adversaries no mercy!

## WEAPONS SHOULD NOT BE NECESSARY

One of the most important aspects of doing business is comfortability. If the people you are doing business with cause you to feel as if a weapon is needed in order for business to be conducted, then maybe you are veering off track, because weapons should not be necessary when doing business with people who display the proper business etiquette. Even if you are involved in business that it would be nice if a weapon was available, for one to be completely necessary would be a telltale sign that maybe the individual or business at hand is not something you want to be associated with.

Anyhow, just because they should not be necessary does not mean you should not take precautions and stay prepared. The thing is that you should do so by the book, to prevent becoming a victim of the pitfalls that otherwise await. If you have already fallen victim and are unable to secure such security legitimately, then you should consider hired security. Now if that is not an option, then return to Chapter 1.

## NEVER UNDERESTIMATE THE OPPOSITION

You can never let your guard down and begin to under-estimate your opposition, or the extent to which they will go to get ahead of you as their competition. You must protect any differences or advantages you have from your opposition and pay close attention to those closest to you and/or your opposition. Never take for granted your accomplishments or advantages and try to always be prepared for a change in the tide.

Just as you would protect your differences and advantages (trademark, trade secrets, business practices, etc., etc.), you should guard yourself against your opposition obtaining personal knowledge on you that could be useful to them at interrupting your operation and/or growth. Of course there are some details you will not be able to keep concealed; only those that are sensitive and/or crucial things that can be contained, all care must be taken to keep them protected and away from exposure.

# 25 RESPECT YOUR COMMUNITY

*If you do not respect your community,*
*how could you ever expect anyone else to*
*respect it, or it to respect you?*
—M.L. Walker Sr.

You will often hear people boast and brag about their neighborhoods, sides of town, cities, or body of people they associate themselves with. You would think they truly loved what they claim to be a representation of, yet in most cases you then see or hear, in some way or another, quite the opposite. Respect for one's community has always been a must in order for one's community to bud and flourish. There is a reason why neighbors manicure their lawns and worry about the upkeep of one another's homes, or all band together to address issues that affect them as a whole.

Communities may consist of multiple different ethnic groups and cultures, yet mostly all will share the same common interest in regards to that stretch of area they all live in and share or the body of people they all embrace as their own. And what is truly interesting about this is that the majority of these individuals may not even know each other or say anything more than hello to one another, yet they all care about their communal environment. Why? Because in a sense your community is an extension of your home and/or family, and as expressed in the quote, if you do not respect it, then how can you expect for anyone else to.

This feeling of responsibility to a community is especially so for those who were raised there, have lived there for quite some time, or have plans of living there for awhile. For instance, let's imagine you see someone blatantly throw trash on the street or sidewalk of your neighborhood. Even though your residence may be a block over, you will more than likely feel some type of pang, as if that person had thrown it on your block, yard, or floor. The same would go for the mistreatment of someone of said community who you would figure shared a form of sanctuary of communal kinship.

Attachments to communities can sometimes last a lifetime. This includes those who are still within it as well as those who are away. These attachments may also spark different levels of responsibility to said communities, yet some form of responsibility all the same. Be it through secretiveness, bias, uppity-ness, honor, or pride, everyone has a way of showing their dedication and fulfilling their presumed responsibility to communities of which they have accepted their place and attachment.

There is much that could be said in regards to community; however, most of it is something you will see play out on a daily basis, and therefore I will spare you all of the extras and go to the things I feel will guide you yourself in regards to all of the other things that could have been listed as well.

## RESPECT THE PAST

A community's history is everything. The bonding, nurturing, and uplifting is what the cornerstones were built on, atop of the blood-soaked soils of those early builders and inhabitants. The sense of pride that grows within those inside a community has at times actually cost people their lives, because once the feeling of belonging sets in, the devotion causes people to literally be prepared to protect such with their life. Surely something that people would willingly risk their lives for has to deserve some type of respect and homage.

The first thing you would have to do is take some time to be brought up to speed on some of the pioneers, hurdles, and accomplishments. Knowing the struggles of a community and how passionate others before you were to preserve and improve it could only be helpful in showing you which direction it was desired for it to go in, is headed in, and what could be done on your part to ensure it's heading in the right direction.

As a youngster it will be up to you to seek out the elders who would be most able to share with you the history. And as elders it would be up to you to sit the young down and give them their and the community's history. Fact is, this would be nurturing for all involved because sometimes we need to take breaks from the world outside of ours for a while to become more in tune with ourselves and the community around us. But yes, take the time to learn more about what it is that you are embracing.

## RESPECT THE LAW

I am not going to encourage you to respect law enforcement, since for the most part they enter such for the wrong reason and with the wrong intentions and abuse the authority with which they are entrusted. However, I am suggesting that you respect the laws of the land and those of your community. And yes, I can understand how even that is not easy and will get no easier with all of the nonsense these governments are enacting as law, which are ridiculous for one reason or another, to the point they have even begun to criminalize normal behavior and felonize minor infractions. Still in all, to respect the laws does not require you to agree with them. In fact, just so we are clear, the form of respect that I am speaking of is reading up on laws and becoming knowledgeable on the things that will affect you and/or others in the community at some point or another. Because being knowledgeable on these laws will allow you and those closest to you to stay on course, not fall victim to the pitfalls, and keep you abreast on what the government's agendas are.

Also, although I do not encourage for you to respect law enforcement, I do encourage you to be respectful in regards to them doing their duties in a professional manner. Respectfully decline to participate in any dealings with them without an attorney present. Respectfully allow them to do their jobs and solve crimes through some form of real evidence as opposed to word of mouth and civilians doing all of the work for them, with none of the pay. Respect the position as a peacekeeper enough to report when they themselves are not respecting you or your community, since respect is a two-way street.

# 26 AVOID DANGEROUS SITUATIONS

*Danger is always one situation away. Avoid
it or allow your fate to be decided by such.*
—M.L. Walker Sr.

It is very rare that we find ourselves in situations which we have not placed ourselves in. So if this tells us nothing else, it tells us that we usually do in fact have a say in the situations that we place ourselves in. Therefore if it is true that we have a say, then why would we ever want to place ourselves in dangerous or compromising positions or situations?

In this chapter it is my hope of getting you to exercise more control over the situations you place yourself and others in. Surely I understand that sometimes there could be a thrill to be found venturing into the unknown or edgier elements; however, if it's not necessary, then why even begin to subject yourself or those around you to the nonsense that could possibly be interjected into your life. Yes, I come from a crime-ridden environment and am thankful for all that I learned, yet the last thing I want is for any of you to have to experience the deceit, treachery, and betrayal of people simply trying to survive, as I have had to in order to be able to provide you with this manual. Nevertheless, it will be on you to weigh your pros and cons and decide what best suits you. What I do know is that strength and character already run through your veins, and there are more than enough avenues to learn how to effectively protect yourselves without having to endanger your lives.

In the plainest terms ever, you simply have to be willing to listen to your inner voice and do your own statistical probability markup, and from there make a conscious decision that you will be able to live with, no matter the outcome. I mean if you decide to make a crime-ridden neighborhood your daily hangout, then there is a great chance that you will find yourself associated with such at some point, be it directly or indirectly, literally or presumptuously. So unless you live there or are a part of that element, why else would you make it a habit of being there? And just for the record, this differs from the "assessing situations" as covered in Chapter 12 "Master Your Surroundings," as in this case you are to attempt to analyze and assess a situation prior to ever actually being in it, in order to prevent you from ever having to be in the situation to begin with. Yet and still, if and when you ever do find yourself in one of those unfortunately dangerous situations (whether you have done your part to avoid it or not), then the issues covered in Chapter 12 would in fact apply.

There are a few more topics that must be covered in this chapter; however, before doing so I would like to ensure that nothing about this should be taken as or used to be judgmental. Dangerous situations can consist of anything and are not restricted to any one ethnic group, area, or form of which it is perilous. And this is why you must be keenly in tune with the things this manual was created to enlighten you to, so that you will be able to sense and pinpoint what is or could turn into a dangerous situation for you.

The following subtitles are things that are closely related to dangerous situations and/or what your response to such should be if you happen to find yourself in the middle of a dangerous situation or interactions that appear to be leading towards such.

## MIND YOUR OWN BUSINESS

Honestly this should be self-explanatory and something you should have been told time and again by those around you, that is if they truly have your best interest and care about your well-being. The truth is that it really just does not pay to go around poking your nose in other people's business. And yes, I get the whole good Samaritan lure; however, I gave you my input regarding wanting to be a hero early on in this manual. This does not mean you abandon all desire to come to the assistance of someone else, only do not make it your prerogative to make other people's business yours. If it is not something or someone you have a vested interest in, then surely it would be best to allow someone who does have a vested interest in the situation or people involved to deal with whatever needs dealing with, however it is to be dealt with.

## KNOW YOUR ENEMY

Hopefully you never have to become enemies with anyone, because it is one thing to be disliked or to not get along with someone, yet a rather deeper thing once you cross over to being an enemy. Becoming an enemy entails that whatever dislike or feud you have been entangled in has now escalated to where it involves harm, and therefore if you make or become an enemy of anyone... you had better know exactly who that enemy is!

Once you have dialed in on exactly who that enemy is, you should find out everything you possibly can about said enemy: where they work, where they live, family structure, where they shop, buy gas, and frequent. You will want to know their vices, who their allies are, as well as their strengths and weaknesses. Most importantly you will need to know how imminent of a threat they are.

Sometimes you will be able to employ others to obtain this insight for you, as you never want to give too much energy to nonsense and foolishness, or to have such taking away from productiveness. Yet other times you will have no other choice but to attend to said affairs yourself. No matter what, you will usually always have to do some type of digging, which may cause you to utilize other sources. Be cautious to shield your identity when possible, and when unable to do so, be sure to tap trustworthy sources. You should always double- or triple-check information that is volunteered, the people who volunteer it, and their reasoning for volunteering it.

## USE FEAR AS A WEAPON

This is not something that should be demonstrated freely, but rather only when completely necessary. It is my belief that you should always prefer to be respected as opposed to feared; however, sometimes I question whether or not I took the correct position. People may have assumed I personally put the latter first, only I simply displayed to what extent I would go to demand the respect I deserve.

Back to fear: it is an emotion that when sincerely felt can literally paralyze a person. When instilling fear into someone, you yourself usually have to be sincere and actually willing to follow through with whatever the threat is, because if you are not, then your subject may sense that you are not and attempt to bluff or simply be stubborn enough to attempt to call what they perceive to be or hope is a bluff.

Ironically, within your utilizing fear as a weapon, you do not want to overdo it and scare them beyond control. When it comes to the options usually available with fear, you should always prefer they take flight as opposed to fight. If there is nowhere to flee, then you want them to concede control of the situation. Nonetheless, it will be up to you to control the level of fear and ultimately the situation.

## DESTROY WHAT IS NECESSARY COMPLETELY

When the time comes that destroying is deemed necessary, then no matter what it is or the reason for destruction being the course of action, be sure to leave no guessing about the finality of that destroyed! Do not overthink it but surely put some type of thought into what you are doing and how it is you plan to complete the task. And if you leave a trail of debris behind, then you have failed to do your job correctly. Leave nothing to guess!

# 27 ALWAYS REMAIN TRUE TO YOURSELF

*By being true to yourself, you will not have to worry whether or not others will or will not be.*
—M.L. Walker Sr.

As you should have realized by now, a lot of what was covered in the previous chapters pertained to being able to remain true to who you are and were born to be. Yet even with that being the case, emphasis is needed. Why? Because in today's way of going about things, insincerity has become the norm, while authenticity has become even more rare than ever! This is why extreme care must be given to protect the integrity of your authenticity, if in fact it is there.

Now I am very aware that the "if in fact it is there" may have caused a bit of a sting inside, and you are wondering what exactly I mean by that, since in your mind everyone is born with it and it is simply up to us to live it. Well, for the most part you would be correct, since as newborn infants we are truly as authentic as we will ever he. However, with every proceeding day, the taint of deception finds its way into our minds and (for the most part) our hearts. And unfortunately, from there, most of us will choose the easiest route by living life in moral turpitude, whereas others will simply be staying true to their nature to live life in the low. Surely you all have met someone who every bit of aura that exudes their circumference spells out that they are nothing more than rotten to the core. Most of you would relate this to being shady, conniving, underhanded, etc., etc. And no, just because a person looks a certain way or gives off this impression does not make it so, yet more times than not, they will live up to it. So this is why the "if it's there" had to be included, because the harsh reality of the matter is that most people in the world, and most people who will pick up this manual, will not be sincere people through and through. Some of you will be striving to become better people, which is truly a good thing and a very possible achievement, while others will seek only to better conceal their insincerity. Either way, the point is that the period of every one of us being in a natural state of pure sincerity is a very brief one. Once as infants and only again if we are fortunate enough to live to the point of being senile (if anything can be fortunate about winding up in such a state, and depending on others to treat you compassionately), though even in that state some will be so stuck in their ways of lower self that they will unconsciously do things that to them are natural, no matter how immoral or deceitful it may actually be.

There are no shortcuts or mental exercises to help make you learn to be true to yourself (or anyone else for that matter); however, I can inform you that the very first steps to even remotely being close to being able to do so is for you to be honest with yourself. You know yourself better than any other person could ever know you, and since I am sure we all can agree on that... if you are not able to look in the mirror and be as blunt and honest with yourself, then you have failed yourself already. In laymen's terms, in order to be able to remain being true to yourself, you will need to be able to be true with yourself to begin with.

As it should already be known, throughout your entire life there will be people who are connected to you, directly or indirectly, who will do everything they can to get you to bend to their will. They will use every means known to man to accomplish their goals of doing such, for whatever their reason may be, yet this is where so many of the previous chapters would come into play (mainly, 1 "Self-Preservation"; 7 "Be Adaptable"; 9 "Never Be Afraid To Stand Alone"; 11 "Control Your Tongue; 13 "Know How To Differentiate"; 14 "Learn From Your And Others' Mistakes"; 15 "Learn The Art Of Reading People"; 16 "Choose Your Partners Carefully"; 17 "Establish Your Allegiances"; 22 "Play Your Hand Accordingly"; 24 "Always Be About Your Business"; and 26 "Avoid Dangerous Situations") because only you know what exactly it is that you truly stand for and to what extent you are actually willing to stand on it. Yet you need to know that there are no grey areas here. Either you are or you are not, and the value you place on such a thing will dictate your final outcome, but just know that if you refuse to remain true to yourself, there is no way possible you could ever begin to expect anyone else to be true to you or anything you stand for or represent.

www.ingramcontent.com/pod-product-compliance
Lightning Source LLC
Chambersburg PA
CBHW072008040426
42447CB00009B/1542

*9 7 8 1 7 3 2 1 1 2 0 0 1 *